Cantonese
Chinese

phrase book & dictionary

Berlitz Publishing

New York   London   Singapore

Contacting the Editors
Every effort has been made to provide accurate information in this publication, but changes are inevitable. The publisher cannot be responsible for any resulting loss, inconvenience or injury. We would appreciate it if readers would call our attention to any errors or outdated information. We also welcome your suggestions; if you come across a relevant expression not in our phrase book, please contact us at: **comments@berlitzpublishing.com**

All Rights Reserved
© 2007 Berlitz Publishing/APA Publications (UK) Ltd.
Berlitz Trademark Reg. U.S. Patent Office and other countries. Marca Registrada. Used under license from Berlitz Investment Corporation.

Eleventh Printing: March 2012
Printed in China

Publishing Director: Mina Patria
Commissioning Editor: Kate Drynan
Editorial Assistant: Sophie Cooper
Translation: updated by Wordbank
Cover Design: Beverley Speight
Interior Design: Beverley Speight
Production Manager: Raj Trivedi
Picture Researcher: Beverley Speight
Cover Photo: © Main image and top row centre image David Henley/APA; top left and bottom left corners Brice Minnigh/APA; Cantonese script images Alex Havret/APA; 'currency' image iStockphoto

Interior Photos: David Henley/APA 1, 41, 108, 119; Alex Havret/APA 14, 16, 21, 29, 50, 58, 62, 65, 67, 69, 73, 75, 81, 95, 97, 98, 111, 131; Ming Tang-Evans/APA 56, 86; A Nowitz/APA 84, 93, 94; Sylvaine Poitau/APA 89; Corrie Wingate/APA 90; Brice Minnigh/APA 105, 133; iStock 136, 139, 141, 142, 148, 150, 154; James Macdonald/APA 168

Contents

Food & Drink

People

Leisure Time

Special Requirements

In an Emergency

Dictionary

Pronunciation

The romanized pronunciation system widely used for Cantonese Chinese is the Yale romanization system. This system is used throughout the phrase book. Not all romanization letters or letter combinations are pronounced as they normally are in English.

A guide to the pronunciation follows.

In addition to the Roman alphabet, Yale romanization also features tonal marks, which repesent six Cantonese tones:

Tone	Mark	Description	Example	Chinese	Translation
1st	‾	high and level tone	**sī**	絲	*silk*
2nd	´	high, rising tone; starts medium in tone, then rises	**sí**	史	*history*
3rd		mid-level tone; flat, with no emphasis	**si**	試	*try*
4th	` h	low, falling tone; starts medium in tone and then falls sharp and strong	**sìh***	時	*time*
5th	´ h	low, rising tone; starts low then rises to medium tone	**síh***	市	*city*
6th	h	low and level tone	**sih***	事	*matter*

*An 'h' is placed after the vowel to indicate low tone.

Initial Consonants

Symbol	Approximate Pronunciation	Example	Pronunciation
gw	like qu in quiet	貴	*gwai*
kw	like k + w	裙	*kwàhn*
ch	between ch in church and ts in cats	叉	*chā*
j	between j in judge and ds in adds	炸	*ja*
m	like pronouncing m without opening the mouth	唔	*m*
ng	like ng in lying but further back in the mouth	我	*ngóh*

The letters b, d, f, g, h, k, l, m, n, p, s, t, w, y are pronounced generally as in English.

Finals

Symbol	Approximate Pronunciation	Example	Pronunciation
a	like a in father	沙	*sā*
e	like ai in fair	遮	*jē*
eu	like er in her	靴	*hēu*
i	like e in me	紙	*jí*
o	like o in dog	我	*ngóh*
u	like oo in cool	苦	*fú*
yu	like pronouncing you with lips pursed	書	*syū*

Symbol	Approximate Pronunciation	Example	Pronunciation
ai	like ei in Fahrenheit	雞	*gāi*
au	like ou in out	夠	*gau*
am	like um in umbrella	心	*sām*
an	like un in under	身	*sān*
ang	like un in uncle	生	*sāng*
ap	like up	十	*sahp*
at	like ut in utmost	實	*saht*
ak	like uck in luck	得	*dāk*
aai	like ai in aisle	街	*gāai*
aau	like ou in foul	教	*gaau*
aam	like am in Guam	三	*sāam*
aan	like aun in aunt	山	*sāan*
aang	like aun in aunt + g	行	*hàahng*
aap	like arp in harp	垃	*laahp*
aat	like art in cart	辣	*laaht*
aak	like ark in bark	肋	*laahk*
ei	like ei in eight	記	*gei*
eng	like e + ng	靚	*leng*
ek	like eck in deck	隻	*jek*
eui	like oi, pruonced with lips rounded	去	*heui*
eun	like en in enable, pronounced with lips rounded	信	*seun*
eut	like eu + t	出	*chēut*
eung	like eu + ng	香	*hēung*
euk	like eu + k	腳	*geuk*
iu	like il in until	笑	*siu*

Symbol	Approximate Pronunciation	Example	Pronunciation
im	like im in impolite	甜	tìhm
in	like in	天	tīn
ing	like ing in sing	星	sīng
ip	like ip in sip	涉	sip
it	like it in sit	洩	sit
ik	like ick in sick	識	sīk
ou	like ou in dough	好	hóu
oi	like oi in oil	開	hōi
on	like on	乾	gōn
ong	like on + g	江	gōng
ot	like ot in lot	渴	hot
ok	like auc in auction	各	gok
ui	like ui in cuisine	杯	būi
un	like oun in wound	半	bun
ut	like oo in wood + t	闊	fut
ung	like one in phone	中	jūng
uk	like oak	讀	duhk
yun	like yu + n	院	yún
yut	like yu + t	月	yuht

Cantonese is spoken in Hong Kong, Macau, Guangdong and Guangxi. There are approximately 64 million speakers of Cantonese in the world. Cantonese speakers can also be found in Malaysia, Vietnam, Singapore, Indonesia and among Chinese immigrants all over the world. Although Cantonese speakers read and write Mandarin Chinese, the Cantonese dialect is different in sentence structure, pronunciation and to a certain extent, grammar and vocabulary. This means that Cantonese speakers speak in one way (Cantonese dialect), but write in another (Mandarin Chinese).

Written Chinese is not a combination of letters but ideograms. Each character represents a syllable of spoken Chinese; more than 80% of Chinese characters are actually compounds of two or more characters.

Chinese in written form can be traditional or simplified. Historically, traditional had been used in Hong Kong. Traditional Chinese has more strokes and is written vertically in columns from right to left or horizontally from left to right. Simplified Chinese has fewer strokes and is written horizontally from left to right. This phrase book features traditional Chinese.

How to use this Book

Sometimes you see two alternatives separated by a slash. Choose the one that's right for your situation.

ESSENTIAL

I'm on vacation [holiday]/ business.	我依家度假/出差。 *ngóh yìh gā douh ga/chēut chāai*
I'm going to...	我要去去… *ngóh yiu heui…*
I'm staying at the...Hotel.	我住喺…酒店。 *ngóh jyuh hái… jáu dim*

Words you may see are shown in YOU MAY SEE boxes.

YOU MAY SEE...

抵達 *dái daaht*	arrivals
離境 *lèih gíng*	departures
認領行李 *yihng líhng hàhng léih*	baggage claim

Any of the words or phrases listed can be plugged into the sentence below.

Somewhere to Stay

Can you recommend...?	你可唔可以介紹…? *néih hó m hó yíh gaai juh…*
a hotel	一間酒店 *yāt gāan jáu dim*
a hostel	一間旅舍 *yāt gāan léuih se*
a campsite	一個營地 *yāt go yìhng deih*

Cantonese Chinese phrases appear in purple.

Read the simplified pronunciation as if it were English. For more on pronunciation, see page 7.

Personal

How old are you?	你幾大年紀? *néih géi daaih nìhn géi*
I'm…	我… *ngóh…*
Are you married?	你結咗婚未? *néih git jó fān meih a*
I'm…	我… *ngóh…*
single/in a relationship	單身/有固定朋 *dāan sān/yáuh gu dihng pàhng yáuh*
engaged/married	訂咗婚/結咗婚 *dihng jó fān/git jó fān*
divorced/separated	離咗婚/分咗居 *leih jó fān/fān jó gēui*
widowed	老公 *m*/老婆 *f* 過咗身 *lóuh gūng//lóuh pòh ?gwo jó fān*

When different gender forms apply, the masculine form is followed by *m*; feminine by *f*

For Numbers, see page 160.

Related phrases can be found by going to the page number indicated.

It is polite to address people with: 先生 *sīn sāang* (Sir), 女士 *néuih sih* (Madam) or 小姐 *síu jé* (Miss).

Information boxes contain relevant country, culture and language tips.

Expressions you may hear are shown in You May Hear boxes.

YOU MAY HEAR…

我講少少英文。
ngóh góng síu síu yīng màhn

我唔識講英文。
ngóh m sīk góng yīng màhn

I only speak a little English.

I don't speak English.

Color-coded side bars identify each section of the book.

Survival

ESSENTIAL

I'm on vacation [holiday]/business.	我依家度假/出差。	*ngóh yìh gā douh ga/ chēut chāai*
I'm going to...	我要去···	*ngóh yiu heui...*
I'm staying at the...Hotel.	我住喺···酒店。	*ngóh jyuh hái...jáu dim*

YOU MAY HEAR...

唔該護照。 *m gōi wuh jiu*	Your passport, please.
你嚟嘅目的係乜野? *néih làih ge muhk dīk haih māt yéh*	What's the purpose of your visit?
你住喺邊度? *néih jyuh hái bīn douh*	Where are you staying?
你留幾耐? *néih làuh géi noih*	How long are you staying?
邊個同你一齊嚟? *bīn go tùhng néih yāt chàih làih*	Who are you here with?

Border Control

I'm just passing through.	我淨係過境。	*ngóh jihng haih gwo gíng*
I'd like to declare...	我想申報···	*ngóh séung sān bou...*
I have nothing to declare.	我唔使申報。	*ngóh m sái sān bou*

YOU MAY HEAR...

使唔使申報？ *sái m sái sān bou*
呢件野你要畀稅。 *nī gihn yéh néih yiu béi seui*
唔該你打開呢個袋。 *m gōi néih dá hōi nī go dói*

Anything to declare?
You must pay duty on this.
Open this bag.

U.S. and U.K. citizens must possess a valid passport and visa, issued by the Chinese authorities, to enter China. Tour groups may be issued group visas; the paperwork in this case would be handled by the travel agency. U.S. and U.K. citizens need a valid passport only if their destination is Hong Kong alone.

Before you arrive in China, you will have to fill out a declaration form listing any valuables in your possession. When you leave China, you may be asked to show that you are taking with you the items listed, except for any items declared as gifts. Contact your consulate for information on obtaining visas and for health requirements and travel advisories.

YOU MAY SEE…

海關 *hói gwāan*	customs
免稅物品 *míhn seui maht bán*	duty-free goods
申報物品 *sān bou maht bán*	goods to declare
不需要申報 *bāt sēui yiu* *sān bou*	nothing to declare
護照檢查 *wuh jiu gím chàh*	passport control
警員 *gíng yùhn*	police

Money

ESSENTIAL

Where's…?	···喺邊度？ *…hái bīn douh*
the ATM	自動提款機 *jih duhng tàih fún gēi*
the bank	銀行 *ngàhn hòhng*
the currency exchange office	貨幣兌換處 *fo baih deui wuhn chyu*
When does the bank open/close?	銀行幾時開門/閂門？ *ngàhn hòhng géi sìh hōi mùhn/sāan mùhn*
I'd like to change dollars/pounds into Hong Kong dollars.	我想將美金/英鎊換成港紙。 *ngóh séung jēung méih gām/yīng bóng wuhn sìhng gong jí*
I'd like to cash traveler's checks [cheques].	我想將旅行支票換成現金。 *ngóh séung jēung léuih hàhng jī piu wuhn sìhng yihn gām*

At the Bank

I'd like to change money/get a cash advance.	我想換錢/預支現金。 *ngóh séung wuhn chín/ yuh jī yihn gām*
What's the exchange rate/fee?	外幣兌換率/費係幾多？ *ngoih baih deui wuhn léut/fai haih géi dō*
I think there's a mistake.	我覺得錯咗。 *ngóh gok dāk cho jó*
I lost my traveler's checks [cheques].	我唔見咗旅行支票。 *ngóh m gin jó léuih hàhng jī piu*
My credit card...	我嘅信用卡··· *ngóh ge seun yuhng kāat...*
was lost	唔見咗 *m gin jó*
was stolen	畀人偷咗 *béi yàhn tāu jó*
doesn't work	唔用得 *m yuhng dāk*
The ATM ate my card.	自動取款機食咗我嘅信用卡。 *jih duhng tàih fún gēi sihk jó ngóh ge seun yuhng kāat*

18

Cash is the preferred method of payment in China. However, most major credit cards are accepted in large shopping malls, stores and banks in Hong Kong and other major cities in China. A location that accepts credit card payment will display a credit card symbol in a visible place.

Traveler's checks are accepted at most large banks, but you may have to pay a fee to cash them. Keep the receipt from the bank at home where your traveler's checks were issued as you may be asked to show it. You can change money at most banks and in some of the larger stores.

YOU MAY SEE…

插入信用卡 *chāap yahp seun yuhng kāat*	insert card here
取消 *chéui sīu*	cancel
清除 *chīng chèuih*	clear
進入 *jeun yahp*	enter
密碼 *maht máh*	PIN
取款 *chéui fún*	withdrawal
從支票帳戶取錢 *chùhng jīpiu wu háu chéui chín*	from checking [current] account
從儲蓄帳戶取錢 *chùhng chyú chūk wuh háuh chéui chín*	from savings account
收據 *sāu geui*	receipt

Chinese currency is 人民幣 *yàhn màhn baih* (Ren Min Bi, RMB), literally, 'people's money', not tradable outside China. Currency used in Hong Kong is 港幣 *góng baih* (Hong Kong dollar). The monetary unit of Hong Kong dollars is the 蚊 *mān* (dollar), which is divided into 毫子 *hòuh jí* (ten cents). Bill denominations include 10, 20, 50, 100, 500, 1000 dollars; coins include 1, 2, 5, 10 dollars; 1 *hòuh jí*, 2 *hòuh jí*, 5 *hòuh jí*. One dollar is equal to 10 *hòuh jí*.

Getting Around

ESSENTIAL

How do I get to…?	我點去…？ *ngóh dím heui…*
Where's…?	…喺邊度？ *…hái bīn douh*
the airport	機場 *gēi chèuhng*
the train [railway] station	火車站 *fó chē jaahm*
the bus station	巴士站 *bā sí jaahm*
the subway [underground] station	地鐵站 *deih tit jaahm*
How far is…?	…有幾遠？ *…yáuh géi yúhn*
Where do I buy a ticket?	我喺邊度買飛？ *ngóh hái bīn douh máaih fēi*
A one-way/ round-trip [return] ticket to…	一張去…嘅單程/雙程飛 *yāt jēung heui…ge dāan chìhng/sēung chìhng fēi*
How much?	幾多錢？ *géi dō chín*
Which…?	邊…？ *bīn…*
gate	個閘口 *go jaahp háu*
line	條線 *tìuh sin*
platform	個月台 *go yuht tòih*
Where can I get a taxi?	我喺邊度可以搵到的士？ *ngóh hái bīn douh hó yíh wándóu dīk sí*
Take me to this address.	將我送到呢個地址。 *jēung ngóh sung dou nīgo deih jí*
Can I have a map?	我可唔可以買一張地圖？ *ngóh hó m hó yíh máaih yāt jēung deih tòuh*

20

Tickets

When's…to Tsimshatsui?	去尖沙咀嘅…係乜野時間？	*heui jīm sā jéui ge…haih māt yéh sìh gaan*
the (first) bus	（第一班）巴士	*(daih yāt bāan) bā sí*
the (next) flight	（下一班）飛機	*(hah yāt bāan) fēi gēi*
the (last) train	（最後一班）火車	*(jeui hauh yāt bāan) fó chē*
Where do I buy a ticket?	我喺邊度買飛？	*ngóh hái bīn douh máaih fēi*
One ticket/two tickets, please.	唔該你畀一張/兩張飛我。	*m gōi néih béi yāt jēung/léuhng jēung fēi ngóh*
For today/tomorrow.	要今日/聽日嘅。	*yiu gām yaht/tīng yaht ge*
A…ticket.	一張…飛。	*yāt jēung…fēi*
one-way	單程	*dāan chìhng*
return-trip	雙程	*sēung chìhng*
first class	頭等艙	*tàuh dáng chōng*
business class	商務艙	*sēung mouh chōng*
economy class	經濟艙	*gīng jai chōng*
How much?	幾多錢？	*géi dō chín*
Is there…discount?	…有冇折？	*…yáuh móuh jit*
a child	細蚊仔	*sai mān jái*
a student	學生	*hohk sāang*

a senior citizen	老人 *lóuh yàhn*
a tourist	遊客 *yàuh haak*
The express bus/ express train, please.	特快巴士/特快火車，唔該。 *dahk faai bā sih/ dahk faai fó chē, m̀ gōi.*
The local bus/train, please.	當地嘅巴士/火車，唔該。 *dōng deih ge bā sih/fó chē, m̀ gōi.*
I have an e-ticket.	我有一張電子飛。 *ngóh yáuh yāt jēung dihn jí fēi*
Can I buy a ticket on the bus/train?	我可唔可以喺巴士/火車上面買飛票？ *ngóh hó m̀ hó yíh hái bā sí/fó chē seuhng mihn máaih fēi*
Do I have to stamp the ticket before boarding?	我係唔係一定要上車前喺車票上蓋章？ *ngóh haih m̀ haih yāt dihng yiu séuhng chē chìhn hái chē piu seuhng koi jēung*
How long is this ticket valid?	呢張飛有效時間係幾耐？ *nī jēung fēi yáuh haauh sìh gaan haih géi noih*
Can I return on the same ticket?	我可唔可以用同一張飛返嚟？ *ngóh hó m̀ hó yíh yuhng tùhng yāt jēung fēi fāan làih*
I'd like to...	我想…我定嘅位。 *ngóh séung…ngóh dehng*
my reservation.	*ge wái*
cancel	取消 *chéui sīu*
change	改變 *gói bin*
confirm	確認 *kok yihng*

For Days, see page 164.

For Time, see page 163.

Plane

Airport Transfer

How much is a taxi to the airport?	去機場坐的士要幾多錢？ *heui gēi chèuhng chóh dīk sí yiu géi dō chín*
To...Airport, please.	唔該你帶我去…機場。 *m̀ gōi néih daai ngóh heui… gēi chèuhng*
My airline is...	我嘅航空公司係… *ngóh ge hòhng hūng gūng sī haih…*

My flight leaves at…	我嘅航班···起飛 *ngóh ge hòhng bāan…héi fēi*
I'm in a rush.	我依家趕時間。 *ngóh yìh gā gón sìh gaan*
Can you take an alternate route?	你可唔可以行第二條路？ *néih hó m hó yíh hàahng daih yih tìuh louh*
Can you drive faster/slower?	你可唔可以揸快/慢啲？ *néih hó m hó yíh jā faai/maahn dī*

YOU MAY HEAR…

你坐邊間航空公司嘅班機？ *néih chóh bīn gāan hòhng hūng gūng sī ge bāan gēi*

What airline are you flying?

國內定係國際航班？ *gwok noih dihng haih gwok jai hòhng bāan*

Domestic or international?

邊一個候機大堂？ *bīn yāt go hauh gēi daaih tòhng*

What terminal?

Many U.S. and U.K. airlines have frequent flights to and from Hong Kong and other major cities in China. Internal flights are also available. Transportation from the airport to the downtown area is available at most international airports.

If you plan on traveling throughout China, it is a good idea to make arrangements in advance. There are a few main tourist information offices that can help you to book tickets, hotels and flights: China International Travel Service (www.cits.net), China Travel Service (www.chinatravelservice.com) and China Youth Travel Sevice (www.chinayouthtravel.com). See page 107 for more.

YOU MAY SEE...

抵達 *dái daaht*	arrivals
離境 *lèih gíng*	departures
認領行李 *yihng líhng hàhng léih*	baggage claim
安全 *ngōn chyùhn*	security
國內航班 *gwok noih hòhng bāan*	domestic flights
國際航班 *gwok jai hòhng bāan*	international flights
辦理登機手續 *baahn léih dāng gèi sáu juhk*	check-in
辦理電子登機手續 *baahn léih dihn jí dāng gèi sáu juhk*	e-ticket check-in
登機口 *dāng gēi háu*	departure gates

Checking In

Where's check-in?	喺邊度辦理登機手續？ *hái bīn douh baahn léih dāng gēi sáu juhk*
My name is...	我叫… *ngóh giu...*
I'm going to...	我要去… *ngóh yiu heui...*
I have...	我有… *ngóh yáuh...*
one suitcase	一個行李箱 *yāt go hàhng léih sēung*
two suitcases	兩個行李箱 *léuhng go hāhng léih sēung*
one piece of hand luggage	一件隨身行李 *yāt gihn chèuih sān hàhng léih*
How much luggage is allowed?	可以帶幾件行李？ *hó yíh daai géi gihn hàhng léih*
Is that pounds or kilos?	係英磅定係公斤？ *haih yīng bóng dihng haih gūng gān*
Which terminal/gate?	邊個候機大堂／登機口？ *bīngo hauh gēi daaih tòhng/dāng gēi háu*

YOU MAY HEAR...

下一個！ *hah yāt go* — Next!

唔該你出示護照/機票。 *m gōi néih chēut sih wuh jiu/gēi piu* — Your passport/ticket, please.

你有冇行李寄艙？ *néih yáuh móuh hàhng léih gei chōng* — Are you checking any luggage?

嗰件隨身行李太大。 *gó gihn chèuih sān hàhng léih taai daaih* — That's too large for a carry-on [piece of hand-luggage].

你係唔係自己打包? *Néih haih m haih jih géi dá bāau* — Did you pack these bags yourself?

有冇人俾嘢你拎? *yáuh móuh yàhn béi yéh néih līng* — Did anyone give you anything to carry?

唔該除鞋 *m gōi chèuih hàaih* — Take off your shoes.

依家…登機。 *yìhgā…dāng gēi* — Now boarding...

I'd like a window/an aisle seat.	我想要窗口/路口位。 *ngóh séung yiu chēung háu/louh háu wái*
When do we leave/arrive?	我哋幾點離開/到？ *ngóh deih géi dím lèih hōi/dou*
Is the flight delayed?	飛機係唔係遲咗？ *fēi gēi haih m haih chìh jó*
How late?	有幾遲？ *yáuh géi chìh*

Luggage

Where is/are...?	…喺邊度？ *...hái bīn douh*
the luggage trolleys	手推車 *sáu tēui chē*
the luggage lockers	行李暫存箱 *hàhng léih jaahm chyùhn sēung*
the baggage claim	認領行李 *yihng líhng hàhng léih*

My luggage has been lost/stolen.	我嘅行李唔見咗/畀人偷咗。	*ngóh ge hàhng léih m gin jó/béi yàhn tāu jó*
My suitcase is damaged.	我嘅手提箱畀人整壞咗。	*ngóh ge sáu tàih sēung béi yàhn jíng waaih jó*

Finding your Way

Where is/are…?	…喺邊度？	*…hái bīn douh*
the currency exchange	換錢	*wuhn chín*
the car hire	租車	*jōu chē*
the exit	出口	*chēut háu*
the taxis	的士	*dīk sí*
Is there…to Guangzhou?	有冇去廣州嘅…？	*yáuh móuh heui gwóng jāu ge…*
a bus	巴士	*bā sí*
a train	火車	*fó chē*
a subway [underground]	地鐵	*deih tit*

For Asking Directions, see page 36.

Train

Where's the train [railway] station?	火車站喺邊度？	*fó chē jaahm hái bīn douh*
How far is…?	…有幾遠？	*…yáuh géi yúhn*
Where is/are…?	…喺邊度？	*…hái bīn douh*
the ticket office	售票處	*sauh piu chyu*
the information desk	訊問處	*sēun mahn chyu*
the luggage lockers	行李暫存箱	*hàhng léih jaahm chyùhn sēung*
the platforms	月台	*yuht tòih*

YOU MAY SEE...

月台 *yuht tòih*	platforms
信息 *seuhn sīk*	information
預定 *yuh dehng*	reservations
候車室 *hauh chē sāt*	waiting room
抵達 *dái daaht*	arrivals
離開 *lèih hōi*	departures

Can I have a schedule [timetable]?	畀一張時間表我好唔好？ *béi yāt jēung sìh gaan bíu ngóh hóu m hóu*
How long is the trip?	要幾耐時間？ *yiu géi noih sìh gaan*
Is it a direct train?	係唔係直到？ *haih m haih jihk dou*
Do I have to change trains?	我使唔使轉車？ *ngóh sái m sái jyun chē*
Is the train on time?	火車準唔準時？ *fó chē jéun m jéun sìh*

Departures

Which track [platform] to...?	邊個月台去…？ *bīn go yuht tòih heui…*
Is this the track [platform]/train to...?	呢個係唔係去…嘅月台/火車？ *nī go haih m haih heui…ge yuht tòih/fó chē*
Where is track [platform]...?	…月台喺邊度？ *…yuht tòih hái bīn douh*
Where do I change for...?	我點樣轉車去…？ *ngóh dím yéung jyun chē heui…*

On Board

Can I sit here/open the window?	我可唔可以坐喺呢度/打開窗？ *ngóh hó m hó yíh chóh hái nī douh/dá hōi chēung*
That's my seat.	嗰個係我嘅位。 *gó go haih ngóh ge wái*
Here's my reservation.	我訂咗呢個位。 *ngóh dehng jó nī go wái*

China has a vast rail network and you can travel by train to almost every Chinese city and town. There are different types of train services available: 快車 *faai chē* (express), 慢車 *maahn chē* (regular) and 直達 *jihk daaht* (non-stop). There are five classes of seats: hard seat, soft seat, hard sleeper, soft sleeper and standing. Buy a ticket at the train station or from one of the ticket offices located throughout the major cities. Before boarding, have your ticket validated by an attendant at the station. There may be machines to validate your tickets in the larger cities. In addition to extensive rail service, Hong Kong, Shenzhen and Guangzhou also have subway systems. Buy your ticket at the subway station from a vending machine and validate it at the ticket machine.

Bus

Where's the bus station?	車站喺邊度？	*chē jaahm hái bīn douh*
How far is it?	有幾遠？	*yáuh géi yúhn*
How do I get to…?	我點樣去…？	*ngóh dím yéung heui…*
Is this the bus to…?	呢架係唔係去…嘅巴士？	*nī ga haih m haih heui…ge bā sí*
Can you tell me when to get off?	你可唔可以話界我知幾時落車？	*néih hó m hó yíh wah béi ngóh jī géi sìh lohk chē*
Do I have to change buses?	我使唔使轉巴士？	*ngóh sái m sái jyun bā sí*
How many stops to…?	到…有幾多個站？	*dou…yáuh géi dō go jaahm*
Stop here, please!	唔該喺呢度停車！	*m gōi hái nī douh tìhng chē*

For Tickets, see page 21.

YOU MAY HEAR...

請大家上車！ *chéng daaih g ā séuhng chē*	All aboard!
唔該車飛。 *m gōi chē fēi*	Tickets, please.
你要喺九龍堂轉車。 *néih yiu hái gáu lùhng tòhng jyun chē*	You have to change at Kowloon Tong.
下一站係尖沙咀。 *hah yāt jaahm haih jīm sā jéui*	Next stop, Tsim Sha Tsui.

Subway

Where's the subway [underground] station?	地鐵站喺邊度？ *deih tit jaahm hái bīn douh*
A map, please.	唔該畀一張地圖我。 *m gōi béi yāt jēung deih tòuh ngóh*
Which line for...?	邊條線去…？ *bīn tiùh sin heui...*
Which direction?	邊個方向？ *bīn go fōng heung*
Do I have to transfer [change]?	我使唔使轉地鐵？ *ngóh sái m sái jyun deih tit*
Is this the subway [underground] to...?	呢架地鐵去唔去…？ *nī ga deih tit heui m heui...*

There are three kinds of bus systems in China: public buses for city transportation, tourist buses for sightseeing and long-distance buses for travel outside of town. Most buses run from 6:00 a.m. to 11:00 p.m daily. In major cities, you can purchase a monthly discounted pass for public buses. Tourist buses, which are available in major cities, may offer flexible fares (especially for groups) so be sure to negotiate with the driver. Long-distance buses in China service practically every small town, including those in remote regions not accessible by train or plane. There is a bus station in almost every town, big and small, where you can buy tickets and find information on schedule, fares and routes. For public and long-distance buses, have your ticket validated by an attendant before boarding. In Hong Kong, you can also pay the fare when you get on the bus or you can buy a prepaid card, 八達通 baat daaht tūng (also known as an octopus card), at train and subway stations; these 'octopus' cards can be used on all types of public transportation throughout the city.

How many stops to…?	到…有幾多個站？	dou…yáuh géi dō go jaahm
Where are we?	我哋喺邊度？	ngóh deih hái bīn douh

For Tickets, see page 21.

YOU MAY SEE…

巴士站 bā sí jaahm	bus stop
唔該有落 m̀h gōi yáuh lohk	request stop
上車／落車 séuhng chē/lohk chē	enter/exit
車票蓋章 chē piu koi jēung	stamp your ticket

Boat & Ferry

When is the ferry to…?	去···嘅渡輪係乜野時間？	*heui… ge douh lèuhn haih māt yéh sìh gaan*
Where are the life jackets?	救生衣喺邊度？	*gau sāng yī hái bīn douh?*
Can I take my car?	我可唔可以攞我部車？	*ngóh hó m hó yíh ló ngóh bouh chē?*
What time is the next sailing?	下一班船幾點?	*hah yāt bāan syùhn géi dím*
Can I book a seat/cabin?	我可唔可以預訂一個座位/艙位？	*ngóh hó m hó yíh yuh dehng yāt go joh waih/chōng waih*
How long is the crossing?	航道有幾長？	*hòhng douh yáuh géi chèuhng*

For Tickets, see page 21.

Major cities in China, including Hong Kong, Guangzhou and Shenzhen, have subway systems. You can purchase one-trip tickets and discounted monthly passes at subway stations; some cities may also offer daily and/or weekend tickets. The ticket booth attendants can provide information on operation times, routes and fares. At some stations, you simply pay and enter; at others, you buy a ticket and have it validated by an attendant before boarding. Large cities often have validation machines. Maps are available from the ticket booth, usually for a fee.

YOU MAY SEE...

救生船 *gau sāng syùhn*	life boat
救生衣 *gau sāng yī*	life jacket

Taxi

Where can I get a taxi?	我喺邊度可以叫的士?	*ngóh hái bīndouh hó yíh giu dīk sí*
Can you send a taxi?	你可唔可以派部的士?	*néih hó m hó yíh paai bouh dīk sih*
Do you have the number for a taxi?	你有冇的士公司電話?	*néih yáuh móuh dīk sí gūng sī dihn wá*
I'd like a taxi now/ for tomorrow at...	我宜家/聽日喺···想叫的士。	*ngóh yìh gā/ tīng yaht hái...séung giu dīk sí*
Pick me up at...	喺···接我。	*hái...jip ngóh*
I'm going to...	我要去···	*ngóh yiu heui...*
this address	呢個地址	*nī go deih jí*
the airport	機場	*gēi chèuhng*

There is regular ferry and boat service between large coastal cities of China as well as along rivers, particularly the Chang Jiang (Yangzi) and Zhu Jiang (Pearl) but not the Huang He (Yellow). Some islands in Guangdong are accessible by ferry. Check with a travel agent or the local ferry terminal for schedules, routes and fares.

There is regular ferry service between Hong Kong island and Kowloon. The Hong Kong ferry is a main tourist attraction because of the renowned night scenery, which includes views of the coastal area of Hong Kong island and Kowloon pennisula. There is also regular ferry service between Hong Kong island and nearby outlying islands.

Taxi service in Hong Kong and most other main cities in China is usually meter-based; in smaller towns or in the countryside, you may need to negotiate a flat fee with the driver. Hail a taxi on the street by raising your arm or from a taxi stand, recognizable by a TAXI sign. There is usually no surcharge for luggage, but a nighttime surcharge may apply. Tipping the taxi driver is not usual in China, but will be happily accepted.

the train [railway] station	火車站	*fó chē jaahm*
I'm late.	我遲咗。	*ngóh chìh jó*
Can you drive faster/slower?	你可唔可以開快/慢啲?	*néih hó m̀ hó yíh hōi faai/maahn dī*
Stop/Wait here.	喺呢度停車/等我。	*hái nī douh tìhng chē/dáng ngóh*
How much?	幾多錢?	*géi dō chín*
You said it would cost…	你講過要…	*néih góng gwo yiu…*
Can I have a receipt?	我可唔可以要收據?	*ngóh hó m̀ hó yíh yiu sāu geui*
Keep the change.	唔使找喇。	*m̀ sái jáau la*

YOU MAY HEAR…

去邊度? *heui bīn douh*	Where to?
地址係乜野? *deih jí haih māt yéh*	What's the address?
有夜間/機場附加費。 *yáuh yeh gāan/gēi chèuhng fuh ga fai*	There's a nighttime/airport surcharge.

Bicycle & Motorbike

I'd like to hire a bicycle/motorcycle.	我想租一架單車/一架電單車。 *ngóh séung jōu yāt ga dāan chē/yāt ga dihn dāan chē*
I'd like to hire a moped.	我想租部電單車。 *ngóh séung jōu bouh dihn dāan chē*
How much per day/week ?	一日/個星期幾多錢？ *yāt yaht/go sīng kèih géi dō chín*
Can I have a helmet/lock?	我可唔可以買一個頭盔/一把鎖？ *ngóh hó m hó yíh máaih yāt go tòuh kwāi/yāt bá só*

Cycling is a popular method of transportation throughout China. Bicycles can be rented in many Chinese towns, either at hotels or bicycle shops. To avoid parking fines and to minimize the risk of having the bicycle stolen, park the bicycle at guarded parking spaces for a small fee.

In Hong Kong, cycling is mainly for recreational purposes. Since the traffic in Hong Kong is extremely busy, it is dangerous to ride bicycles within congested city areas.

Car Hire

Where's the car hire?	喺邊度租車？ *hái bīn douh jōu chē*
I'd like...	我想要… *ngóh séung yiu…*
a cheap/small car	一架平啲/細啲嘅車 *yāt ga pèhng d ī/sai dī ge chē*
an automatic/a manual	手波/自動波 *sáu bō/jih duhng bō*
air conditioning	冷氣 *láahng hei*
a car seat	兒童安全座位 *yìh tùhng ngō chyùhn joh wái*

How much...?	…幾多錢？ *...géi dō chín*
per day/week	每日/個星期 *múih yaht/go sīng kèih*
per kilometer	每公里 *múih gūng léih*
for unlimited mileage	不限里程 *bāt haahn léih chìhng*
with insurance	有保險 *yáuh bóu hím*
Are there any discounts?	有冇折？ *yáuh móuh jit*

Fuel Station

Where's the fuel station?	油站喺邊度？ *yàuh jaahm hái bīn douh*
Fill it up.	唔該入滿。 *m gōi yahp múhn*
... euros, please.	… 歐元，唔該。 *...áu yùhn, mh gōi*
I'll pay in cash/ by credit card.	我用現金/信用卡畀錢。 *ngóh yuhng yihn gām/seun yuhng kāat béi chín*

For Numbers, see page 160.

YOU MAY HEAR...

你有冇國際車牌？ *néih yáuh móuh gwokjai chē pàaih*	Do you have an international driver's license?
唔該你出示你嘅護照。 *m gōi néih chēut sih néih ge wuhtjiu*	Your passport, please.
你想唔想買保險？ *néih séung m séung máaih bóu hím*	Do you want insurance?
我需要按金。 *ngóh sēui yiu ngon gām*	I'll need a deposit.
喺呢度簽你嘅名。 *hái nī douh chīm néih ge méng*	Sign here.

Car rental agencies are available only in major cities for driving within the city limits. You can, however, hire a driver for a few hours, a day or longer at a rate that you can negotiate. Talk to your hotel concierge about safe rental options.

Asking Directions

Is this the way to…?	呢度係唔係去…嘅路？	*nī douh haih m haih heui…ge louh*
How far is it to…?	去…有幾遠？	*heui…yáuh géi yúhn*
Where's…?	…喺邊度？	*…hái bīn douh*
…Street	…街	*…gāai*
this address	呢個地址	*nī go deih jí*
the highway [motorway]	高速公路	*gōu chūk gūng louh*
Can you show me on the map?	你可唔可以喺地圖上面指畀我睇？	*néih hó m hó yíh hái deih tòuh seuhng mihn jí béi ngóh tái*
I'm lost.	我盪失路。	*ngóh dohng sāt louh*

YOU MAY SEE...

汽油 *hei yàuh*	gas [petrol]
有鉛 *yáuh yùhn*	leaded
無鉛 *mòuh yùhn*	unleaded
普通 *póu tūng*	regular
超級 *chīu kāp*	super
優質 *yāu jāt*	premium
柴油 *chàaih yàuh*	diesel
自助服務 *jih joh fuhk mouh*	self-service
全面服務 *chyùhn mihn fuhk mouh*	full-service

YOU MAY HEAR...

一直向前 *yāt jihk heung chìhn*	straight ahead
左邊 *jó bīn*	left
右邊 *yauh bī*	right
喺/轉過街角 *hái/jyun gwo gāai gok*	on/around the corner
對面 *deui mihn*	opposite
後面 *hauh mihn*	behind
旁邊 *pòhng bīn*	next to
後 *hauh*	after
北/南 *bāk/nàahm*	north/south
東/西 *dūng/sāi*	east/west
喺交通燈嗰度 *hái gāau tūng dāng gó douh*	at the traffic light
喺十字路口 *hái sahp jih louh háu*	at the intersection

Parking

Can I park here?	我可唔可以停喺呢度？ *ngóh hó m hó yíh tìhng hái nī douh*
Where's...?	···喺邊度？ *...hái bīn douh*
the parking garage	車房 *chē fòhng*
the parking lot [car park]	停車場 *tìhng chē chèuhng*
the parking meter	停車計時器 *tìhng chē gai sìh hei*
How much...?	幾多錢···？ *géi dō chín...*
per hour	每個鐘頭 *múih go jūng tàuh*
per day	每日 *múih yaht*
overnight	通宵 *tūng sīu*

YOU MAY SEE...

停 *tìhng*	stop
讓 *yeuhng*	yield [give way]
不准駛入 *bāt jéun sái yahp*	do not enter
禁區 *gam kēui*	restricted area
進入 *jeun yahp*	enter
轉左 *jyun jó*	turn left
轉右 *jyun yauh*	turn right
停車場 *tìhng chē chèuhng*	parking lot [car park]
入口 *yahp háu*	entrance
出口 *chēut háu*	exit
行人路 *hàahng yàhn louh*	pedestrian road

Breakdown & Repair

My car broke down/ won't start.	我嘅車壞咗/唔行得。 *ngóh ge chē waaih jó/m hàahng dāk*
Can you fix it?	你可唔可以整好？ *néih hó m hó yíh jíng hóu*
When will it be ready?	幾時可以整好？ *géi sìh hó yíh jíng hóu*
How much?	幾多錢？ *géi dō chin*
I have a puncture/ flat tyre (tire).	我嘅車胎穿/爆咗。 *ngóh ge chē tāi chyūn / baau jó*

Accidents

There was an accident.	有意外。 *yáuh yi ngoih*
Call an ambulance/ the police.	打電話叫一架救護車/警察。 *dá dihn wá giu yāt ga gau wuh chē/gíng chaat*

Places to Stay

ESSENTIAL

Can you recommend a hotel?	你可唔可以推薦一間酒店？ *néih hó m hó yíh tēui jin yāt gāan jáu dim*
I have a reservation.	我定咗房。 *ngóh dehng jó fóng*
My name is...	我嘅名係… *ngóh ge méng haih…*
Do you have a room...?	有冇…嘅房間？ *yáuh móuh…ge fòhnggāan*
for one/two	一/兩個人 *yāt/léuhng go yàhn*
with a bathroom	有沖涼房 *yáuh chūng lèuhng fóng*
with air conditioning	有冷氣 *yáuh láahng hei*
For...	住… *jyuh…*
tonight	今晚 *gām máahn*
two nights	兩晚 *léuhng máahn*
one week	一個星期 *yāt go sīng kèih*
How much?	幾多錢？ *géi dō chín*
Is there anything cheaper?	有冇平啲嘅嘅？ *yáuh móuh pèhng dī ge*
When's check-out?	幾點退房？ *géi dím teui fóng*
Can I leave these in the safe?	我可唔可以將呢啲野留喺保險箱？ *ngóh hó m hó yíh jēung nī dī yéh láuh hái bóu hím sēung*
Can I leave my bag?	我可唔可以將呢個袋留低？ *ngóh hó m hó yíh jēung nī go dói làuh dāi*
I'll pay in cash/by credit card.	我用現金/信用卡畀錢。 *ngóh yuhng yihn gām/seun yuhng kāat béi chín*
Can I have my receipt?	可唔可以畀收據我？ *hó m hó yíh béi sāu geui ngóh*

Somewhere to Stay

Can you recommend…?	你可唔可以介紹…？	*néih hó m̀ hó yíh gaai siuh…*
a hotel	一間酒店	*yāt gāan jáu dim*
Can you recommend…?	你可唔可以介紹…？	*néih hó m̀ hó yíh gaai siuh…*
a hostel	一間旅舍	*yāt gāan léuih se*
a campsite	一個營地	*yāt go yìhng deih*
a bed and breakfast	一間有早餐嘅酒店	*yāt gāan yáuh jóu chāan ge jáu dim*
What is it near?	呢度離邊度近？	*nī douh lèih bīn douh káhn*
How do I get there?	我點去嗰度呢？	*ngóh dím heui gó douh nē*

At the Hotel

I have a reservation.	我訂咗。	*ngóh dehng jó*
My name is…	我嘅名係…	*ngóh ge méng haih…*
Do you have a room…?	有冇…嘅房？	*yáuh móuh…ge fóng*
with a bathroom	有沖涼房	*yáuh chūng lèuhng fóng*
with a toilet	有洗手間	*yáuh sái sáu gāan*
with a shower	沖涼房	*chūng lèuhng fóng*
with air conditioning	有冷氣	*yáuh láahng hei*
that's smoking/ non-smoking	嗰間係吸煙/非吸煙房	*gó gāan haih kāp yīn/fēi kāp yīn fóng*
For…	住…	*jyuh…*
tonight	今晚	*gām máahn*
two nights	兩晚	*léuhng máahn*
a week	一個星期	*yāt go sīng kèih*

Do you have…?	你有冇…? *néih yáuh móuh…*
a computer	電腦 *dihn nouh*
an elevator [a lift]	電梯 *dihn tāi*
(wireless) internet service	（無線）互聯網服務 *(mòuh sin) wuh lyùhn móhng fuhk mouh*
room service	客房送餐服務 *haak fóng sung chāan fuhk mouh*
a TV	電視機 *dihn sih gēi*
a pool	游泳池 *yàuh wihng chìh*
a gym	健身房 *gihn sān fóng*
I need…	我需要… *ngóh sēui yiu…*
an extra bed	加床 *gā chòhng*
a cot	一張BB床 *yāt jēung bìh bī chòhng*
a crib	一個搖籃 *yāt go yìuh láam*

Price

How much per night/week?	每晚/星期幾多錢? *múih máahn/sīng kèih géi dō chín*
Does that include breakfast/sales tax [VAT]?	包唔包早餐/銷售稅? *bāau m bāau jóu chāan/sīu sauh seui*
Are there any discounts?	有冇折? *yáuh móuh jit*

Preferences

Can I see the room?	我可唔可以睇吓間房？	*ngóh hó m hó yíh tái háh gāan fóng*
I'd like…room.	我想要一間···嘅房。	*ngóh séung yiu yāt gāan…ge fóng*
a better	好啲	*hóu dī*
a bigger	大啲	*daaih dī*
a cheaper	平啲	*pèhng dī*
a quieter	靜啲	*jihng dī*
I'll take it.	我要呢間房。	*ngóh yiu nī gāan fóng*
No, I won't take it.	唔要，我唔要呢間房。	*m yiu ngóh m yiu nī gāan fóng*

YOU MAY HEAR…

唔該你出示你嘅護照／信用卡。
m gōi néih chēut sih néih ge wuh jiu/seun yuhng kāat

填好呢份表格。 *tìhn hóu nī fahn bíu gaak*

喺呢度簽名。 *hái nī douh chīm méng*

Your passport/credit card, please.

Fill out this form.

Sign here.

Questions

Where's…?	···喺邊度？	*…hái bīn douh*
the bar	酒吧	*jáu bā*
the bathroom [toilet]	浴室	*yuhk sāt*
the elevator [lift]	電梯	*dihn tāi*

Hotels, 酒店 *jáu dim*, in China range from budget to luxury. Many quality hotels belong to international chains with service and prices to match. Larger hotels may feature an English-speaking service attendant who holds room keys, handles laundry, sells cigarettes, snacks, drinks and postcards and offers general assistance. If available, postal, phone and foreign exchange services are usually located on the first floor. In general, hotels are ranked from three to five stars and most add on a 10-15% service charge. It's best to look for places to stay in advance, especially if you plan on visiting China during the prime tourist months of May, September and October.

Worth mentioning are the famous, well-preserved hotels dating from colonial times: Peninsula Hotel Hong Kong, Island Shang-ri-la Hong Kong, Garden Hotel Guangzhou and White Swan Guangzhou. Reservations for these must be made well in advance.

Can I have...?	我可唔可以要…? *ngóh hó m hó yíh yiu...*
a blanket	一張毯 *yāt jēung jīn*
an iron	一個熨斗 *yāt go tong dáu*
the room key/ key card	房間鎖匙/鎖匙卡 *fòhng gāan só sìh/só sìh kāat*
a pillow	一個枕頭 *yāt go jám tàuh*
soap	一舊番鹼 *yāt gauh fāan gáan*
toilet paper	廁紙 *chi jí*
a towel	一條毛巾 *yāt tìuh mòuh gān*
Do you have an adapter for this?	你有冇呢個火牛? *néih yáuh móuh nī go fó ngàuh*
How do I turn on the lights?	我點樣開燈? *ngóh dím yéung hōi dāng*

Can you wake me at…?	你可唔可以…叫醒我？ *néih hó m hó yíh…giu séng ngóh*
Can I leave these in the safe?	我可唔可以將呢啲野留喺保險箱？ *ngóh hó m hó yíh jēung nī dī yéh làuh hái bóu hím sēung*
Is there mail [post]/ a message for me?	有冇郵件/留言畀我？ *yáuh móuh yàuh gín/ làuh yìhn béi ngóh*
What time do you lock up?	幾點鎖門？ *géi dím só mùhn*
Do you have a laundry service?	你哋有冇洗衫服務？ *néih deih yáuh móuh sái sāam fuhk mouh*

For Time, see page 163.

Problems

| There's a problem. | 有問題。 *yáuh mahn tàih* |
| I lost my key/ key card. | 我唔見咗鎖匙/鎖匙卡。 *ngóh m gin jó só sìh/ só sìh kāat* |

YOU MAY SEE…

推/拉 *tēui/lāai*	push/pull
沖涼房 *chūng lèuhng fóng*	restroom [toilet]
花灑 *fā sá*	shower
電梯 *dihn tāi*	elevator [lift]
樓梯 *làuh tāi*	stairs
洗衣 *sái yī*	laundry
請勿打擾 *chíng maht dá yíu*	do not disturb
防火門 *fòhng fó mùhn*	fire door
(緊急)出口 *(gán gāp) chēut háu*	(emergency) exit
電話叫醒 *dihn wá giu séng*	wake-up call

The voltage used in China is 220. You will need an adapter for any appliances and electronics brought into the country.

I've locked my key/ key card in the room.	我嘅鑰匙/鑰匙卡鎖咗入房。	*ngóh ge só sīh/só sīh kā só jó yahp fóng.*
There's no hot water/ toilet paper.	冇熱水/廁紙。	*móuh yiht séui/chi jí*
The room is dirty.	房好烏糟。	*fóng hóu wū jōu*
There are bugs in the room.	房有蟲。	*fóng yáuh chùhng*
...doesn't work.	…唔得。	*...m dāk*
Can you fix...?	你可唔可以整…?	*néih hó m hó yíh jíng...*
the air conditioning	冷氣	*láahng hei*
the fan	風扇	*fūng sin*
the heat	暖氣	*nyúhn hei*
the light	燈	*dāng*
the TV	電視	*dihn sih*
the toilet	洗手間	*sái sáu gāan*
I'd like another room.	我想換房。	*ngóh séung wuhn fóng*

Checking Out

When's check-out?	幾點退房?	*géi dím teui fóng*
Can I leave my bag here until...?	我可唔可以將個袋留喺呢度…?	*ngóh hó m hó yíh jēung go dói làuh hái nī douh...*
Can I have an itemized bill/a receipt?	你可唔可以畀一張詳細帳單/ 收據我?	*néih hó m hó yíh béi yāt jēung chèuhng sai jeung dāan/sāu geui ngóh*

| I think there's a mistake. | 我認為錯咗。 *ngóh yihng wàih cho jó* |
| I'll pay in cash/ by credit card. | 我用現金/信用卡畀錢。 *ngóh yuhng yihn gām/seun yuhng kāat béi chín* |

For Time, see page 163.

Renting

I reserved an apartment/a room.	我訂咗一個單位/一間房。 *ngóh dehng jó yāt go dāan wái/yāt gāan fóng*
My name is...	我嘅名係··· *ngóh ge méng haih...*
Can I have the key/key card?	可唔可以畀鎖匙/鎖匙卡我? *hó m̀ hó yíh béi só sìh/só sìh kāat ngóh*
Are there...?	有冇···? *yáuh móuh...*
dishes	碟 *díp*
pillows	枕頭 *jám tàuh*
sheets	床單 *chòhng dāan*
towels	毛巾 *mòuh gān*
utensils	餐具 *chāan geuih*
When do I put out the bins/recycling?	我幾時倒垃圾/回收垃圾? *ngóh géi sìh dóu laahp saap/ wùih sāu laahp saap*
...is broken.	···壞咗。 *...waaih jó*
Can you fix...?	你可唔可以整···? *néih hó m̀ hó yíh jíng...*
the air conditioner	冷氣 *láahng hei*
the dishwasher	洗碗機 *sái wún gēi*
the freezer	雪櫃 *syut gwaih*
the heater	暖氣 *nyúhn hei*
the microwave	微波爐 *mèih bō lòuh*
the refrigerator	冰箱 *bīng sēung*
the stove	爐 *lòuh*
the washing machine	洗衣機 *sái yī gēi*

Domestic Items

I need...	我需要…	ngóh sēui yiu...
an adapter	一個火牛	yāt go fó ngàuh
aluminum foil	錫紙	sehk jí
a bottle opener	瓶瓶器	hōi pìhng hei
a broom	一把帚把	yāt bá sou bá
a can opener	罐頭刀	gun táu dōu
cleaning supplies	清潔用品	chīng git yuhng bán
a corkscrew	開酒器	hōi jáu hei
detergent	清潔劑	chīng git jāi
dishwashing liquid	洗潔精	sái git jīng
bin bags	垃圾袋	laahp saap dói
a lightbulb	一個燈膽	yāt go dāng dáam
matches	一啲火柴	yāt dī fó chàaih
a mop	一個拖板	yāt go tō báan
napkins	一啲餐巾	yāt dī chāan gān
paper towels	紙巾	jí gān
plastic wrap [cling film]	保鮮紙	bóu sīn jí
a plunger	泵	bām
scissors	一把較剪	yāt bá gaau jín
a vacuum cleaner	一架吸塵機	yāt ga kāp chàhn gēi

For In the Kitchen, see page 77.

For Oven Temperatures, see page 167.

At the Hostel

Is there a bed available?	有冇床？	yáuh móuh chòhng
Can I have...?	可唔可以畀…我？	hó m hó yíh béi…ngóh
a single/ double room	一間單人/雙人房	yāt gāan dāan yàhn/sēung yàhn fóng

Hostels in China provide inexpensive accommodation options. Beds in dorm-style rooms are the least costly choice; private rooms ranging from singles to rooms for six or more may also be available but will usually need to be reserved in advance. Be prepared to pay in cash at hostels and other budget accommodations; credit cards are often not accepted, especially at locations in small towns. Hostels in China associated with Hostelling International accept online reservations; these often offer internet service and more. Visit the Hostelling International website at www.hihostels.com for details.

a blanket	一張毯	*yāt jēung jīn*
a pillow	一個枕頭	*yāt go jám tàuh*
sheets	床單	*chòhng dāan*
a towel	一條毛巾	*yāt tìuh mòuh gān*
Do you have lockers?	有冇衣櫃？	*yáuh móuh yī gwaih*
When do you lock up?	幾點鎖門？	*géi dím só mùhn*
Do I need a membership card?	使唔使會員證？	*sái m̀ sái wúih yùhn jing*
Here's my International Student Card.	呢個係我嘅國際學生證。	*nī go haih ngóh ge gwok jai hohk sāang jing*

Going Camping

Can I camp here?	我可唔可以喺呢度露營？	*ngóh hó m̀ hó yíh hái nī douh louh yìhng*
Where's the campsite?	營地喺邊度？	*yìhng deih hái bīn douh*
What is the charge per day/week?	每日/星期幾多錢？	*múih yaht/sīng kèih géi dō chín*
Are there…?	有冇…？	*yáuh móuh…*
cooking facilities	烹飪設施	*pāang yahm chit sī*

YOU MAY SEE...

飲用水 *yám yuhng séui*	drinking water
禁止野營 *gam jí yéh yìhng*	no camping
禁止生火/燒烤 *gam jí sāng fó/sīu hāau*	no fires/barbecues

electric outlets	電掣	*dihn jai*
laundry facilities	洗衣設施	*sái yī chit beih*
showers	花灑	*fā sá*
tents for hire	出租嘅帳篷	*chēut jōu jeung fùhng*

For Domestic Items, see page 47.

For In the Kitchen, see page 77.

Camping is fairly uncommon in China; most campsites are located near a nature preserve or other attractions. Check with your travel agent or the concierge at your hotel for more information.

Communications

ESSENTIAL

Where's an internet cafe?	網吧喺邊度？ *móhng bā hái bīn douh*
Can I access the internet/check e-mail?	我可唔可以上網/查電子郵件？ *ngóh hó m hó yíh séung móhng/chàh dihn jí yáuh gín*
How much per hour/half hour?	每個/半個鐘頭幾多錢？ *múih go/bun go jūng tàuh géi dō chín*
How do I connect/log on?	我點樣上網？ *ngóh dím yéung séuhng móhng*

49

A phone card, please.	唔該畀一張電話卡我。 *m gōi béi yāt jēung dihn wá kāat ngóh*
Can I have your phone number?	可唔可以畀你嘅電話號碼我？ *hó m hó yíh béi néih ge dihn wá houh máh ngóh*
Here's my number/e-mail.	呢個係我嘅電話號碼/電郵地址。 *nī go haih ngóh ge dihn wá houh máh/dihn yàuh deih jí*
Call/E-mail me.	打電話/發電郵畀我。 *dá dihn wá/faat dihn yàuh béi ngóh*
Hello. This is…	你好，我係… *néih hóu ngóh haih…*
Can I speak to…?	我可唔可以同…傾？ *ngóh hó m hó yíh tùhng…kīng*
Can you repeat that?	你可唔可以重複一次？ *néih hó m hó yíh chùhng fūk yāt chi*
I'll call back later.	我等一陣再打電話嚟。 *ngóh dáng yāt jahn joi dá dihn wá làih*
Bye.	再見。 *joi gin*
Where's the post office?	郵局喺邊度？ *yàuh gúk hái bīn douh*
I'd like to send these to…	我想將呢啲野送到… *ngóh séung jēung nī dī yéh sung dou…*

Online

Where's an internet cafe?	網吧喺邊度？	*móhng bā hái bīn douh*
Does it have wireless internet?	有冇無線上網？	*yáuh móuh mòuh sin séung móhng*
What is the WiFi password?	無線網絡嘅密碼係乜野？	*mòuh sin móhng lohk ge maht máh haih māt yéh*
Is the WiFi free?	無線網絡係唔係免費嘅？	*mòuh sin móhng lohk haih m haih míhn fai gàh*
Do you have bluetooth?	你有冇藍牙？	*néih yáuh móuh làahm ngàh*
How do I turn the computer on/off?	點樣開/關電腦？	*dím yéung hōi/gwāan dihn nóuh*
Can I…?	我可唔可以…？	*ngóh hó m hó yíh…*
access the internet	上網	*séuhng móhng*
check e-mail	查電郵	*chàh dihn yàuh*
print	列印	*liht yan*
use any computer	用電腦	*yuhng dihn nóuh*
plug in/charge my laptop/iPhone/iPad/BlackBerry?	插入電源/幫我個手提電腦/iPhone/iPad/Blackberry充電？	*chaap yahp dihn yùhn/bōng ngóh go sáu tàih dihn nóuh/iPhone/iPad/Blackberry chūng dihn*
access Skype?	用Skype	*yuhng Skype*
How much per (half) hour?	每(半)個鐘頭幾多錢？	*múih (bun) go jūng tàuh géi dō chín*
How do I…?	點樣…？	*dím yéung…*
connect/disconnect	連接/斷線	*lìhn jip/tyúhn sin*
log on/log off	登錄/退出	*dāng luhk/teui chēut*
type this symbol	輸入呢個符號	*syū yahp nī go fùh hóu*

What's your e-mail?	你嘅電郵係乜野？ *néih ge dihn yàuh haih māt yéh*
My e-mail is...	我嘅電郵係… *ngóh ge dihn yàuh haih...*
Do you have a scanner?	你有冇掃描器？ *néih yáuh móuh sou mìuh hei*

Social Media

Are you on Facebook/Twitter?	你有冇註冊Facebook/Twitter？ *néih yáuh móuh jyu chaak Facebook/Twitter*
What's your user name?	你個用戶名係乜嘢？ *néih go yuhng wuh mèhng haih māt yéh*
I'll add you as a friend.	我想加你為好友。 *ngóh séung gā néih wàih hóu yáuh*
I'll follow you on Twitter.	我會係Twitter關注你。 *ngóh wúih haih Twitter guān jyu néih*
Are you following...?	你關注緊...？ *néih guān jyu gán...*
I'll put the pictures on Facebook/Twitter.	我想將幅相放上Facebook/Twitter. *ngóh séung jēung fūk seung fong séuhng Facebook/Twitter*
I'll tag you in the pictures.	我會係相片裡面標你。 *ngóh wúih haih seung pin léuih mihn bīu néih*

Phone

A phone card/prepaid phone, please.	唔該畀一張電話卡/預付電話卡我。 *m gōi béi yāt jēung dihn wá kāat/yuh fuh dihn wá kāat ngóh*
How much?	幾多錢？ *géi dō chin*
Can I recharge/buy minutes for this phone?	我可唔可以幫呢個電話加錢/買多啲分鐘？ *ngóh hó m hó yíh bōng nī go dihn wá gā chín/máaih dō dī fān jūng*
Where's the pay phone?	公用電話係邊度？ *gūng yuhng dihn wá haih bīn douh*

YOU MAY SEE...

關閉 *gwāan bai*	close
刪除 *sāan chèuih*	delete
電子郵件 *dihn jí yàuh gín*	e-mail
退出 *teui chēut*	exit
幫助 *bōng joh*	help
聊天 *lìuh tīn*	instant messenger
互聯網 *wuh lyùhn móhng*	internet
登錄 *dāng luhk*	login
新（信息）*sān (seun sīk)*	new (message)
開/關 *hōi/gwāan*	on/off
打開 *dá hōi*	open
列印 *liht yan*	print
保存 *bóu chyùhn*	save
送 *sung*	send
用戶名/密碼 *yuhng wuh méng/maht máh*	username/password
無線上網 *mòuh sin séuhng móhng*	wireless internet

What's the area/country code for...?	…區號/國家代碼係乜野？ …*kēui houh/gwok gā doih máh haih māt yéh*
What's the number for Information?	訊問台號碼係幾多號？ *sēun mahn tòih houh máh haih géi dō houh*
I'd like the number for...	我想要…嘅號碼。 *ngóh séung yiu…ge houh máh*
I'd like to call collect [reverse the charges].	我想打對方付費電話。 *ngóh séung dá deui fōng fuh fún dihn wá*
My phone doesn't work here.	我嘅電話喺呢度唔用得。 *ngóh ge dihn wá hái nī douh m yuhng dāk*

Internet-access centers and cafes can be found in major cities in China. Many hotels offer computer and internet facilities in their business centers as well as wireless internet access in private rooms, usually for a fee.

What network are you on?	你用緊乜嘢網絡？	*néih yuhng gán māt yéh móhng lohk*
Is it 3G?	呢個係唔係3G？	*nī go haih m haih 3G*
I have run out of credit/minutes.	我嘅電話費/分鐘已經用曬。	*ngóh ge dihn wá fai / fān jūng yíh gīng yuhng saai*
Can I buy some credit?	我可唔可以充值？	*ngóh hó m hó yíh chūng jihk*
Do you have a phone charger?	你有冇手機充電器？	*néih yáuh móuh sáu gēi chūng dihn hei*

YOU MAY HEAR...

你係邊位？ *néih haih bīn wái*	Who's calling?
唔該等一等。 *m gōi dáng yāt dáng*	Hold on.
我幫你接。 *ngóh bōng néih jip*	I'll put you through.
佢唔喺度/接緊另一個電話。 *kéuih m hái douh/jip gán lihng yāt go dihn wá*	He/She is not here/on another line.
你使不使留言？ *néih sái m sái làuh yìhn*	Would you like to leave a message?
之後/十分鐘後再打。 *jī hauh/sahp fān jūng hauh joi dá*	Call back later/in 10 minutes.
佢可唔可以打電話畀你？ *kéuih hó m hó yíh dá dihn wá béi néih*	Can he/she call you back?
你幾號電話？ *néih géi houh dihn wá*	What's your number?

Public phones can be found in most cities in China but rarely in remote areas. These phones are usually coin-operated; some may be designed for use with credit cards or phone cards, which can be purchased from grocery stores, convenience stores or newsstands. For a better rate, make international calls from the calling centers or stalls in larger cities. Local calls within China and at hotels are often free.

Calls from Hong Kong to other cities in China and Macau are considered long-distance. Avoid making international calls from hotels, where high surcharges are added.

For national calls, dial 0 + area code + the phone number.

For calls to the U.S. or Canada, dial 00 + 1 + area code + phone number.

For calls to the U.K., dial 00 + 44 + area code + phone number.

Can I have your number?	可唔可以畀你嘅電話號碼我？	*hó m hó yíh béi néih ge dihn wá houh máh ngóh*
Here's my number.	呢個係我嘅號碼。	*nī go haih ngóh ge houh máh*
Please call/text me.	唔該你打電話/發短信畀我。	*m gōi néih dá dihn wá/faat dyún seun béi ngóh*
I'll call/text you.	我會打電話/發短信畀你。	*ngóh wúih dá dihn wá/faat dyún seun béi néih*

Telephone Etiquette

Hello. This is…	你好。我係…	*néih hóu ngóh haih…*
Can I speak to…?	我可唔可以同…傾？	*ngóh hó m hó yíh tùhng… kīng*
Extension…	唔該你轉…	*m gōi néih jyun…*
Speak louder/ more slowly, please.	唔該你大聲/慢慢講。	*m gōi néih daaih sēng/ maahn máan góng*

Can you repeat that?	你可唔可以再講？ *néih hó m hó yíh joi góng*
I'll call back later.	我之後再打。 *ngóh jī hauh joi dá*
Bye.	再見。 *joi gin*

For Numbers, see page 160.

Fax

Can I send/receive a fax here?	呢度可唔可以發/接傳真？ *nī douh hó m hó yíh faat/sāu chyùhn jān*
What's the fax number?	傳真號係幾多？ *chyùhn jān houh máh haih géi dō*
Please fax this to...	唔該你將呢個傳真畀… *m gōi néih jēung nī go chyùhn jān béi...*

Post

| Where's the post office/mailbox [postbox]? | 郵局/郵箱喺邊度？ *yàuh gúk/yàuh sēung hái bīn douh* |
| A stamp for this postcard/letter to... | 一張將呢張明信片/ *yāt jēung jēung nī jēung mìhng seun pín/fūng seun gei dou...ge yàuh piu* |

YOU MAY HEAR…

填好海關申報表。
tìhn hóu hói gwāan sān bou bíu

價值係幾多？ *ga jihk haih géi dō*

裏面裝啲乜野？ *léuih mihn jōng dī māt yéh*

Fill out the customs declaration Form.

What's the value?

What's inside?

How much?

Send this package by airmail/express.

A receipt, please.

幾多？ *géi dō*

用航空/用快件寄呢個包裹 *yuhng hòhng hūng/yuhng faai gín gei nī go bāau gwó*

唔該你畀收據我。 *m gōi néih béi sāu geui ngóh*

Post offices can be found throughout China. They normally provide express, registered, overnight and general mail service. Additionally, they may also take payment on behalf of utility companies. Online postal services are available; you can mail your packages, track their status, wire money, order merchandise and pay utility bills.

Food & Drink

ESSENTIAL

Can you recommend a good restaurant/bar?	你可唔可以介紹一間好嘅餐廳/酒吧？ *néih hó m hó yíh gaai siuh yāt gāan hóu ge chāan tēng/jáu bā*
Is there a traditional Chinese/an inexpensive restaurant nearby?	附近有冇傳統嘅中國/唔貴嘅餐廳？ *fuh gahn yáuh móuh chyùhn túng ge jūng gwok/m gwai ge chāan tēng*
A table for one/two, please.	唔該畀一/兩人嘅檯我。 *m gōi béi yāt/léuhng yàhn ge tói ngóh*
Can we sit...?	我哋可唔可以坐喺…？ *ngóh deih hó m hó yíh chóh hái...*
here/there	呢度/嗰度 *nī douh/gó douh*
outside	外面 *ngoih mihn*
in a non-smoking area	禁煙區 *gam yīn kēui*
I'm waiting for someone.	我等緊人。 *ngóh dáng gán yàhn*
Where's the restroom [toilet]?	洗手間喺邊度？ *sái sáu gāan hái bīn douh*
A menu, please.	唔該你畀菜牌我。 *m gōi néih béi choi páai ngóh*
What do you recommend?	你介紹乜野菜呢？ *néih gaai siuh māt yéh choi nē*
I'd like...	我想要… *ngóh séung yiu...*
Some more..., please.	唔該你再畀一啲…我。 *m gōi néih joi béi yāt dī...ngóh*

59

Enjoy your meal!	慢用！ *maahn yuhng*
The check [bill], please.	唔該埋單。 *m gōi màaih dāan*
Is service included?	包唔包服務費？ *bāau m bāau fuhk mouh fai*
Can I pay by credit card?	我可唔可以用信用卡畀錢？ *ngóh hó m hó yíh yuhng seun yuhng kāat béi chín*
Can I have a receipt?	我可唔可以要一張收據？ *ngóh hó m hó yíh yiu yāt jēung sāu geui*
Thank you!	多謝！ *dō jeh*

Where to Eat

Can you recommend…?	你可唔可以介紹…？ *néih hó m hó yíh gaai siuh…*
a restaurant	一間餐廳 *yāt gāan chāan tēng*
a bar	一間酒吧 *yāt gāan jáu bā*
a cafe	一間咖啡室 *yāt gāan ga fē sāt*
a fast-food place	一間快餐店 *yāt gāan faai chāan dim*
a snack bar	一間小食店 *yāt gāan síu sihk dim*
a teahouse	一間茶樓 *yāt gāan chàh làuh*
a cheap restaurant	一間平價餐廳 *yāt gāan pèhng ga chāan tēng*
an expensive restaurant	一間貴價餐廳 *yāt gāan gwai ga chāan tēng*
a restaurant with a good view	一間風景好嘅餐廳 *yāt gāan fūng gíng hóu ge chāan tēng*
an authentic/a non-touristy restaurant	一間味道正宗/非旅遊觀光嘅餐廳 *yāt gāan meih douh jing jūng/fēi léuih yàuh gūn gwōng ge chāan tēng*

Authentic Chinese food should be one of the highlights of your trip. By Chinese tradition, food should be filling and have a healing effect; a Chinese meal is based on balance. Because of size of the country, Chinese cuisine varies greatly from region to region. The main styles are:

Beijing (Northern) cuisine

Wheat, not rice, is the staple in northern China, so Beijing cuisine is comprised mainly of noodles, steamed bread and dumplings. Beijing is the place to order Peking duck, a roasted, crisy-skinned duck wrapped in wafer-thin pancake with spring onions and sweet bean sauce.

Cantonese (Southern) cuisine

The majority of Chinese restaurants outside of China feature Cantonese-style cooking, so you will likely be familiar with the dishes and flavors. Steaming and stir-frying are the signatures of Cantonese cooking; these methods preserve the food's natural colors, flavors and vitamins. Rice, steamed or stir-fried, is the traditional accompaniment to a Cantonese-style meal.

Hunan (Central) cuisine

Chili pepper is a popular spice here, as in the neighboring Sichuan region, home of Szechuan cuisine. Hunan cuisine is known for rich sweet-and-sour sauces. Smoked and cured food is also popular.

Shanghai (Eastern) cuisine

Seafood and vegetable dishes abound, since this cuisine is based around the coastal areas of Shanghai. Be sure to sample the steamed freshwater crab, honey-fried eel, yellowfish and sautéed shrimp.

Szechuan (Western) cuisine

This province is well-known for its hot, peppery dishes. Food is not just spicy; Szechuan cooking combines a number of flavors: bitter, sweet, tart and sour.

Reservations & Preferences

I'd like to reserve a table…	我想訂一張···嘅檯。	*ngóh séung dehng yāt jēung…ge tói*
for two	兩個人	*léuhng go yàhn*
for this evening	今晚	*gām māan*
for tomorrow at…	聽日···	*tīng yaht…*
A table for two, please.	唔該畀一張兩個人嘅檯我。	*m gōi béi yāt jēung léuhng go yàhn ge tói ngóh*
We have a reservation.	我哋有訂檯。	*ngóh deih yáuh dehng tói*
My name is…	我嘅名係···	*ngóh ge méng haih…*
Can we sit…?	我哋可唔可以坐喺···?	*ngóh deih hó m hó yíh chóh hái…*
here/there	呢度/嗰度	*nī douh/gó douh*
outside	外面	*ngoh mihn*
in a non-smoking area	禁煙區	*gam yīn kēui*
by the window	近窗口	*gahn chēung háu*
in the shade	樹蔭下	*syuh yam hah*
in the sun	太陽下	*taai yèuhng hah*
Where are the toilets?	洗手間喺邊度?	*sái sáu gāan hái bīn douh*

YOU MAY HEAR...

你有冇訂枱？	néih yáuh móuh dehng tói	Do you have a reservation?
幾多人？	géi dō yàhn	How many?
吸煙區定係禁煙區？	kāp yīn kēui dihng gam yīn kēui	Smoking or non-smoking?
你可以叫野未？	néih hó yíh giu yéh meih	Are you ready to order?
你想食乜野呢？	néih séung sihk māt yéh nē	What would you like?
我介紹…	ngóhgaai siuh…	I recommend…
慢慢食。	maahn máan sihk	Enjoy your meal.

How to Order

Waiter/Waitress!	伙記！	fó gei
We're ready to order.	我哋可以叫野喇。	ngóh deih hó yíh giu yéh la
The wine list, please.	唔該畀酒牌我。	m gōi béi jáu páai ngóh
I'd like…	我想要…	ngóh séung yiu…
a bottle of…	一樽…	yāt jēun…
a carafe of…	一碴…	yāt jā…
a glass of…	一杯…	yāt būi…
The menu, please.	唔該你畀菜牌我。	m gōi néih béi choi páai ngóh
Do you have a menu in English/children's menu?	你係唔係有英文菜牌/兒童菜牌？	néih haih m haih yáuh yīng màhn choi páai/yìh tùhng choi páai
Do you have a fixed-price menu?	你有冇固定價格嘅菜單？	néih yáuh móuh gu dihng ga gaak ge choi dāan
What do you recommend?	你介紹乜野？	néih gaai siuh māt yéh
What's this?	呢啲係乜野？	nī dī haih māt yéh
What's in it?	裏面有乜野？	léuih mihn yáuh māt yéh

Is it spicy?	辣唔辣?	*laaht m laaht*
I'd like…	我想要…	*ngóh séung yiu…*
More…, please.	唔該我想再要…	*m gōi ngóh séung joi yiu…*
With/Without…, please.	有/冇…唔該	*yáuh/móuh…m gōi*
I can't have…	我唔食得…	*ngóh m sihk dāk…*
rare	嫩肉	*nyuhn yuhk*
medium	半生熟	*bun sāang suhk*
well-done	全熟	*chyùhn suhk*
It's to go [take away].	我要拎走。	*ngóh yiu nīng jáu*

64

YOU MAY SEE…

附加費 *fuh gā fai*	cover charge
固定價格 *gu dihng ga gaak*	fixed-price
菜單 *choi dāan*	menu
當日菜單 *dōng yaht choi dāan*	menu of the day
(不) 包括服務費	service (not) included
(bāt) bāau kwut fuhk mouh fai	
配菜 *pui choi*	side dishes
特色菜 *dahk sīk choi*	specials

Cooking Methods

baked	烤	*hāau*
boiled	煮	*jyú*
braised	燜	*mān*
creamed	提取乳脂	*tàih chéui yúh jī*
diced	切成細塊	*chit sìhng sai faai*
fileted	去骨切片	*heui gwāt chit pín*
fried	煎	*jīn*
grilled	烤	*hāau*
poached	水煮	*séui jyú*

roasted	烤 *hāau*
sautéed	炒 *cháau*
smoked	薰 *fān*
steamed	蒸 *jīng*
stewed	燉 *dahn*
stuffed	有餡 *yáuh háam*

Dietary Requirements

I'm...	我係... *ngóh haih...*
diabetic	糖尿病患者 *tòhng liuh behng waahn jé*
lactose intolerant	乳糖過敏者 *yúh tòhng gwo mán jé*
vegetarian	素食者 *sou sihk jé*
vegan	素食者 *sou sihk jé*
I'm allergic to...	我對...敏感。 *ngóh deui...máhn gám*
I can't eat...	我唔食得... *ngóh m sihk dāk...*
dairy	乳製品 *yúh jai bán*
gluten	麵筋 *mihn gān*
nuts	硬殼果 *ngaahng hok gwó*
pork	豬肉 *jyū yuhk*
shellfish	貝類 *bui leuih*
spicy foods	辣 *laaht*
wheat	麵 *mihn*

Is it halal/kosher?	呢啲係唔係清真食品/猶太食品？ *nī dī haih m haih chīng jān sihk bán/yàuh taai sihk bán*
Do you have…?	你有冇…? *néih yáuh móuh*
skimmed	脫脂嘅 *tyut jī ge*
whole milk	全脂奶 *chyùhn jī náaih*
soya milk	豆漿 *dauh jēung*

Dining with Children

Do you have children's portions?	你哋有冇兒童餐？ *néih deih yáuh móuh yìh tùhng chāan*
A highchair/child's seat, please.	唔該畀一張高凳/BB凳我。 *m gōi béi yāt jēung gōu dang/bìh bī dang ngóh*
Where can I feed/change the baby?	我喺邊度可以餵BB/幫BB換尿片？ *ngóh hái bīn douh hó yíh wai bìh bī/bōng bìh bī wuhn liuh pín*
Can you warm this?	你可唔可以加熱？ *néih hó m hó yíh gā yiht*

How to Complain

How much longer will our food be?	仲要幾耐時間幫我哋上菜？ *juhng yiu géi noih sìh gaan bōng ngóh deih séung choi*
We can't wait any longer.	我哋唔可以再等喇。 *ngóh deih m hó yíh joi dáng la*
We're leaving.	我哋要走喇。 *ngóh deih yiu jáu la*
I didn't order this.	我冇叫呢碟菜。 *ngóh móuh giu nī dihp choi*
I ordered…	我叫咗… *ngóh giu jó…*
I can't eat this.	呢個唔食得。 *nī go m sihk dāk*
This is too…	呢個太… *nī go taai…*
cold/hot	凍/熱 *dung/yiht*
salty/spicy	鹹/辣 *hàahm/laaht*
tough/bland	硬/淡 *ngaahng/táahm*
This isn't clean/fresh.	呢個唔乾淨/新鮮。 *nī go m gōn jehng/sān sīn*

Paying

The check [bill], please.	埋單。	*màaih dāan*
Separate checks [bills], please.	分開畀。	*fān hōi béi*
It's all together.	一齊畀。	*yāt chàih béi*
Is service included?	包唔包服務費？	*bāau m bāau fuhk mouh fai*
What's this amount for?	呢啲係乜野費用？	*nī dī haih māt yéh fai yuhng*
I didn't have that. I had…	我冇食呢個。我食嘅係…	*ngóh móuh sihk nī go ngóh sihk ge haih…*
Can I have an itemized bill/ a receipt?	你可唔可以畀一張詳細帳單/ 收據我？	*néih hó m hó yíh béi yāt jēung chèuhng sai jeung dāan/sāu geui ngóh*
That was delicious!	呢個好好食！	*nī go hóu hóu sihk*
I've already paid.	我已經俾咗錢。	*ngóh yíh gīng béi jó chín*

Tipping is not expected nor is it compulsory in China, though, in Hong Kong, it is fairly common. Service charges may apply in some restaurants, especially those that offer private rooms. You won't see tax included on the bill; there is no sales tax in China.

Meals & Cooking

Breakfast

bacon	鹹肉	*hàahm yuhk*
bread	麵包	*mihn bāau*
butter	牛油	*ngàuh yàuh*
cereal	麥片	*mahk pín*
cheese	芝士	*jī sí*
coffee/tea...	···咖啡/茶 ...	*ga fē/chàh*
black	黑	*hāk*
decaf	無咖啡因嘅	*mòuh ga fē yān ge*
with milk	加牛奶	*gā ngàuh náaih*
with sugar	加糖	*gā tòhng*
with artificial sweetener	加代糖	*gā doih tòhng*
deep-fried dough sticks	油炸鬼	*yàuh ja gwái*
egg, fried	煎蛋	*jīn dáan*
egg, hard-/soft-boiled	蛋煮得老/嫩	*dáan jyú dāk lóuh/nyuhn*
egg, hard-boiled in tea-leaf water	茶葉蛋	*chàh yihp dáan*
jam	果占	*gwó jīm*

The Chinese tend to eat early. Breakfast, 早餐 *jóu chāan*, is usually served from 6:00 to 8:00 a.m. and lunch, 晏晝 *ngaan jau*, from 11:00 a.m. to 1:00 p.m. You probably won't be able to order dinner, 晚飯 *máahn faahn*, past 8:00 p.m., except in the south, where social life continues until late in the evening. Chinese meals are enjoyed in a group. Tables often have revolving platforms so the various dishes can be shared; using chopsticks lengthens the reach.

Continental breakfast is served at most hotels that cater to Europeans and Americans. If you prefer a Chinese breakfast, your meal will usually be comprised of rice or wheat porridge, to which almost anything can be added, such as fried dough or salted fish. Noodle soup with pieces of pork and/or vegetables is another popular Chinese breakfast.

jelly	啫厘	*jē léi*
…juice	…汁	*…jāp*
apple	蘋果	*pìhng gwó*
grapefruit	西柚	*sāi yáu*
orange	橙	*cháang*
milk	牛奶	*ngàauh náaih*
oatmeal	麥皮	*mahk pèih*
omelet	菴列	*ngām liht*
rice porridge	粥	*jūk*
sausage	香腸	*hēung chéung*
sesame seed cake	芝麻燒餅	*jī màh sīu béng*
soy milk	豆奶	*dauh náaih*

steamed bun	饅頭 *maahn tàuh*
steamed, stuffed bun	包 *bāau*
toast	多士 *dō sí*
yogurt	乳酪 *yúh lohk*
water	水 *séui*

Appetizers

chicken feet	鳳爪 *fuhng jáau*
cold jellyfish in sauce	涼拌海蜇皮 *lèuhng buhn hói jit pèih*
cold stewed beef in sauce	鹵牛肉 *lóuh ngàuh yuhk*
crispy vinegar cucumber	涼拌黃瓜 *lèuhng buhn wòhng gwā*
pickles	泡菜 *paau choi*
preserved egg	皮蛋 *pèih dáan*
shrimp with salt and pepper	椒鹽蝦 *jīu yìhm hā*
sliced ham	火腿 *fó téui*
smoked meat	薰肉 *fān yuhk*
spring roll	春卷 *chēun gyún*
steamed bun	蒸包 *jīng bāau*
steamed dumplings	蒸餃 *jīng gáau*

Chinese appetizers are ordered before a meal. In many restaurants, you can order a platter with a selction of mostly cold dishes.

Soup

…soup	⋯湯 …tōng
bean curd	豆腐 dauh fuh
chicken	雞 gāi
corn and egg	粟米蛋 sūk máih dáan
egg drop	蛋花 daahn fā
hot and sour	酸辣 syūn laaht
meat, seafood and egg	三鮮 sāam sīn
pork	肉絲 yuhk sī
seafood	海鮮 hói sīn
spare rib	排骨 pàaih gwāt
squid	魷魚 yàuh yú
tomato	蕃茄 fāan ké
vegetable	菜 choi

When in China, you may wish to follow Chinese etiquette. Sip your soup directly from the soup bowl or use the ceramic soup spoon provided. Elbows remain on the table and bowls are lifted off the table while enjoying the soup.

Fish & Seafood

clam	蜆 hín
cod	鱈魚 syut yú
crab	蟹 háaih
crucian carp	鯽魚 jāk yú
grass carp	草魚 chóu yú
hairtail	帶魚 daai yú
halibut	大比目魚 daaih béi muhk yú

herring	鯡魚 *pàaih yú*
lobster	龍蝦 *lùhng hā*
octopus	章魚 *jēung yùh*
oyster	蠔 *hòuh*
salmon	三文魚 *sāam màhn yú*
sea bass	鱸魚 *lòuh yú*
shrimp	蝦 *hā*
silver carp	鰱魚 *lìhn yú*
sole	板魚 *báan yú*
squid	魷魚 *yàuh yú*
swordfish	劍魚 *gim yú*
trout	鱒魚 *jēun yú*
tuna	金槍魚 *gām chōng yú*

Meat & Poultry

beef	牛肉 *ngàuh yuhk*
chicken	雞肉 *gāi yuhk*
cured pork	鹹肉 *hàahm yuhk*
duck	鴨肉 *ngaap yuhk*
ham	火腿 *fó téui*
heart (pork)	(豬) 心 *(jyū) sām*
kidney (pork)	(豬) 腰 *(jyū) yīu*
lamb	羊肉 *yèuhng yuhk*
liver	豬肝 *jyū gōn*
oxen entrails	牛雜 *ngàuh jaahp*
oxen tripe	牛柏葉 *ngàuh paak yihp*
pork	豬肉 *jyū yuhk*
pork tripe	豬肚 *jyū tóuh*
rabbit	兔肉 *tou yuhk*
sausage	香腸 *hēung chéung*
spare ribs	豬扒 *jyū pá*
steak	牛扒 *ngàuh pá*

Vegetables & Staples

asparagus	露筍	*louh séun*
broccoli	西蘭花	*sāi làahn fā*
cabbage	椰菜	*yèh choi*
carrot	紅蘿蔔	*hùhng lòh baahk*
cauliflower	菜心	*choi sām*
celery	芹菜	*kàhn choi*
Chinese cabbage	白菜	*baahk choi*
Chinese long bean	荷蘭豆	*hòh lāan dáu*
Chinese water spinach	通菜	*tūng choi*
corn	粟米	*sūk máih*
eggplant [aubergine]	矮瓜	*ngái gwā*
garlic	蒜	*syun*
green bean	扁豆	*bín dáu*
leaf mustard	芥菜	*gaai choi*
lettuce	生菜	*sāang choi*
mushroom	蘑菇	*mòh gū*
noodles	麵	*mihn*
nori (type of seaweed)	紫菜	*jí choi*
olive	橄欖	*gaam láam*

The proper way to eat a bowl of rice is to hold the bowl up with one hand and push the rice into your mouth with chopsticks. Do not stick the chopsticks upright into a bowl of rice; this is considered an ominous sign as it resembles incense sticks burned for funerals or at shrines. When you have finished your meal, rest the chopsticks across the top of the bowl or place them on the table.

pea	豆	*dáu*
potato	薯仔	*syùh jái*
radish	蘿蔔	*lòh baahk*
red/green pepper	紅/青椒	*hùhng/chēng jīu*
rice	米	*máih*
scallion	大蔥	*daaih syun*
seaweed	海帶	*hói daai*
soy bean	黃豆	*wòhng dáu*
spinach	菠菜	*bō choi*
tofu	豆腐	*dauh fuh*
tomato	蕃茄	*fāan ké*
vegetable	菜	*choi*

Fruit

apple	蘋果	*pìhng gwó*
apricot	杏	*hahng*
banana	香蕉	*hēung jīu*
cherry	車厘子	*chē lèih jí*
Chinese dates	棗	*jóu*
crab apple	山碴	*sāan jā*
fruit	生果	*sāang gwó*
grape	提子	*tàih jí*

grapefruit	西柚 *sāi yáu*
kiwi	奇異果 *kèih yih gwó*
lemon	檸檬 *nìhng mūng*
lime	青檸 *chēng níng*
longan fruit	龍眼 *lùhng ngáahn*
lychee	荔枝 *laih jī*
mandarin orange	柑 *gām*
mango	芒果 *mōng gwó*
melon	蜜瓜 *maht gwā*
orange	橙 *cháang*
peach	桃 *tóu*
pear	梨 *léih*
pineapple	菠籮 *bō lòh*
plum	李 *léih*
pomegranate	石榴 *sehk láu*
red bayberry	楊梅 *yèuhng múi*
strawberry	草莓/士多啤厘 *chóu múi/sih dō bē léi*

The Chinese rarely finish a meal with dessert but, instead, have fruit. In general, sweets are eaten as snacks. You can buy desserts at bakeries and teahouses and in some supermarkets.

Dessert

| mixed fruit | 生果 *sāang gwó* |
| sweetened red bean paste | 紅豆沙 *hùhng dáu sā* |

Sauces & Condiments

salt	鹽 *yìhm*
pepper	胡椒 *wùh jīu*
mustard	芥末 *gaai muht*
ketchup	蕃茄醬 *fāan kē jeung*

At the Market

Where are the trolleys/baskets?	手推車/購物籃喺邊度？ *sáu tēui chē/kau maht láam hái bī douh*
Where is…?	…喺邊度？ *…hái bīn douh*
I'd like some of that/this.	我想要嗰個/呢個。 *ngóh séung yiudī gó go/nī go*
Can I taste it?	我可唔可以試吓？ *ngóh hó m hó yíh si háh*
I'd like…	我想要… *ngóh séung yiu…*
a kilo/ half-kilo of…	一公斤/半公斤… *yāt gūng gān/bun gūng gān…*
a liter of…	一升… *yāt sīng…*
a piece/slice of…	一塊… *yāt faai…*
More./Less.	多啲/少啲。 *dō dī/síu dī*
How much?	幾多錢？ *géi dō chín*

YOU MAY HEAR...

我可唔可以幫你？ *ngóh hó m hó yíh bōng néih* — Can I help you?

你想要乜野？ *néih séung yiu māt yéh* — What would you like?

仲要唔要第二啲？ *juhng yiu m yiu daih yih dī* — Anything else?

嗰啲係港幣。 *gó dī haih góng baih* — That's...Hong Kong dollars.

Where do I pay?	我喺邊度畀錢？	*ngóh hái bīn douh béi chín*
A bag, please.	唔該畀一個袋我。	*m gōi béi yāt go dói ngóh*
I'm being helped.	有人幫我喇。	*yáuh yàhn bōng ngóh la*

In the Kitchen

bottle opener	開瓶器	*hōi pìhng hei*
bowl	碗	*wún*
can opener	罐頭刀	*gun táu dōu*
ceramic spoon	湯羹	*tōng gāng*
clay pot	沙鍋	*sā wō*
corkscrew	開酒器	*hōi jáu hei*

In major cities in China, you'll find supermarkets selling a variety of goods, often imported, as well as food items. Most food shopping is done at local markets, where fresh meat, fish, fruit and vegetables can be found. Small grocery stores and convenience stores sell food items such as spices and sauces. You may also be able to purchase cigars and liquor at these stores.

cup	杯 *būi*
fork	叉 *chā*
frying pan	鑊 *wohk*
glass	玻璃杯 *bō lēi būi*
knife	餐刀 *chāan dōu*
measuring cup	量杯 *lèuhng būi*
measuring spoon	量羹 *lèuhng gāng*
napkin	餐巾 *chāan gān*
plate	碟 *díp*
pot	鍋 *wō*
spatula	鏟 *cháan*
spoon	瓷羹 *chìh gāng*
steamer	蒸鍋 *jīng wō*
wok	鑊 *wohk*

YOU MAY SEE...

過期日 *gwo kèih*	expiration date
卡路里 *kā louh léih*	calories
無脂肪 *mòuh jī fōng*	fat free
需冷藏 *sēui láahng chòhng*	keep refrigerated
含有微量… *hàhm yáuh mèih leuhng…*	may contain traces of…
微波爐可用 *mèih bō lòuh hó yuhng*	microwaveable
喺…之前出售 *hái…jī chìhn chēut sauh*	sell by…
適合素食者 *sīk hahp sou sihk jé*	suitable for vegetarians

Drinks

ESSENTIAL

The wine list please.	唔該畀酒牌我。	*m gōi béi jáu páai ngóh*
What do you recommend?	你介紹乜野?	*néih gaai siuh māt yéh*
I'd like a bottle/glass of red/white wine.	我想要一樽/杯紅/白酒。	*ngóh séung yiu yāt jēun/būi hùhng/baahk jáu*
Another bottle/glass, please.	唔該再畀一樽/杯我。	*m gōi joi béi yāt jēun/būi ngóh*
I'd like a local beer.	我想飲當地嘅啤酒。	*ngóh séung yám dōng deih ge bē jáu*
Can I buy you a drink?	我可唔可以請你飲?	*ngóh hó m hó yíh chéng néih yám*
Cheers!	乾杯!	*gōn būi*
A coffee/tea, please.	唔該畀一杯咖啡/茶我。	*m gōi béi yāt būi ga fē/chàh ngóh*
Black.	黑	*hāk*
With…	加…	*gā…*
milk	牛奶	*ngàuh náaih*
sugar	糖	*tòhng*
artificial sweetener	代糖	*doih tòhng*
A…, please.	唔該畀一杯…我。	*m gōi béi yāt būi…ngóh*
juice	果汁	*gwó jāp*
soda	蘇打水	*sō dá séui*
sparkling/ still water	有汽/蒸餾水	*yáuh hei/jīng lauh séui*
Is the water safe to drink?	呢啲水可唔可以飲?	*nī dī séui hó m hó yíh yám*

Non-alcoholic Drinks

coffee	咖啡	*ga fē*
cola	可樂	*hó lohk*
hot chocolate	熱朱古力	*yiht jyū gū līk*
juice	果汁	*gwó jāp*
...tea	...茶	*...chàh*
green	綠	*luhk*
jasmine	茉莉花	*muht léih fā*
lemon	檸檬	*nìhng mūng*
milk	奶	*náaih*
oolong	烏龍	*wū lúng*
milk	牛奶	*ngàuh náaih*
soda	蘇打水	*sō dá séui*
soymilk	豆奶	*dauh náaih*
sparkling/still water	有汽/蒸餾水	*yáuh hei/jīng lauh séui*

Tea is the most popular beverage in China. Although teahouses are not as common as they once were, they are still an ideal location to sample the traditional drink, enjoyed without milk or sugar. In most hotel rooms you will find flasks with hot water and green or black teabags.

Ground coffee is hard to find, though instant coffee is generally available.

Do not drink water directly from the tap. Instead, try mineral water or Chinese soft drinks which are generally very sweet and are sold everywhere. Soy milk is very popular but cow's milk can be found in some supermarkets.

YOU MAY HEAR...

我可唔可以請你飲野？	*ngóh hó m hó yíh chéng néih yám yéh*	Can I get you a drink?
加牛奶定係加糖？	*gā ngàuh náaih dihng haih gā tòhng*	With milk or sugar?
有汽水定係蒸餾水？	*yáuh hei séui dihng haih jīng lauh séui*	Sparkling or still water?

Aperitifs, Cocktails & Liqueurs

brandy	白蘭地酒	*baahk làan déi jáu*
Chinese liqueurs	白酒	*baahk jáu*
gin	氈酒	*jīn jáu*
rum	林酒	*làm jáu*
scotch	蘇格蘭威士忌酒	*sōu gaak làahn wāi sih géi*
tequila	龍舌蘭酒	*lùhng sit làahn jáu*
vodka	伏特加酒	*fuhk dahk gā jáu*
whisky	威士忌酒	*wāi sih géi jáú*

Beer

beer	啤酒 *bē jáu*
bottled/draft	樽/生 *jēung/sāang*
dark/light	黑/淡 *hāk/táahm*
local/imported	當地/進口 *dōng deih/jeun háu*
Tsingtao® beer	青島啤酒 *chīng dóu bē jáu*
lager/pilsener	淡啤/捷克黃啤 *táahm bē/jiht hāk wòhng bē*
non-alcoholic	唔含酒精 *m hàhm jáu jīng*

Wine

wine	葡萄酒 *pòuh tòuh jáu*
champagne	香檳 *hēung bān*
red/white	紅酒/白酒 *hùhng jáu/baahk jáu*
table	餐酒 *chāan jáu*
sparkling	汽酒 *hei jáu*
dessert wine	飯後甜酒 *faahn hauh tìhm jáu*
dry/sweet	乾/甜 *gōn/tìhm*

Though the Chinese are not widely known for their alcoholic drinks, there is a surprisingly large choice on offer. Chinese wine is generally sweet and has been produced in China for thousands of years. Each region has its own speciality, usually made from rice, fruit, flowers or herbs.

Tsingtao® is a popular Chinese beer, brewed from the spring water of the Laoshan mountain. You may wish to try a local beer too as each region has its own.

Chinese liqueurs are often infused with local favorites such as bamboo leaves, chrysanthemum and cloves. The most famous spirits include 茅台酒 *màauh tòih jáu* and 五粮液 *ngh lèuhng yihk*.

On the Menu

almond	杏仁	*hahng yàhn*
anchovy	鯷魚	*sìh yúh*
aperitif	開胃酒	*hōi waih jáu*
apple	蘋果	*pìhng gwó*
apricot	杏	*hahng*
artificial sweetener	代糖	*doih tòhng*
asparagus	露筍	*louh séun*
avocado	牛油果	*ngàuh yàuh gwó*
banana	香蕉	*hēung jīu*
bass	鱸魚	*lòuh yú*
bay leaf	月桂葉	*yuht gwai yihp*
bean	豆	*dáu*
bean sprout	芽菜	*ngàh choi*
beef	牛肉	*ngàuh yuhk*
beer	啤酒	*bē jáu*
brandy	白蘭地酒	*baahk lāan déi jáu*
bread	麵包	*mihn bāau*
breast (of chicken)	雞胸肉	*gāi hūng yuhk*
broth	湯	*tōng*
butter	牛油	*ngàuh yàuh*
buttermilk	乳酪	*yúh lohk*
cabbage	椰菜	*yèh choi*
cake	蛋糕	*daahn gōu*
candy [sweets]	糖	*tóng*
caramel	焦糖	*jīu tòhng*
caraway	茴茜	*yìhm sāi*
carrot	蘿蔔	*lòh baahk*
cashew	腰果	*yīu gwó*

cauliflower	菜心 *choi sām*
celery	芹菜 *kàhn choi*
cereal	穀物 *gūk maht*
cheese	芝士 *jī sí*
cherry	士多啤厘 *sih dō bē léi*
chervil	細葉芹 *sai yihp kàhn*
chestnut	栗子 *leuht jí*
chicken	雞肉 *gāi yuhk*
chili pepper	辣椒 *laaht jīu*
Chinese dates	棗 *jóu*
Chinese liquor	白酒 *baahk jáu*
chives	香蔥 *hēung chūng*
chocolate	朱古力 *jyū gū lihk*
chop	斬 *jáam*
chopped meat	肉餡 *yuhk háam*
cider	蘋果汁 *pìhng gwó jāp*
cilantro [coriander]	香菜 *hēung choi*
cinnamon	肉桂 *yuhk gwai*
clam	蜆 *hín*
clove	丁香 *dīng hēung*
coconut	椰子 *yèh jí*

cod	鱈魚	*syut yú*
coffee	咖啡	*ga fē*
consommé	清燉肉湯	*chīng dahn yuhk tōng*
cookie [biscuit]	曲奇	*kūk kèīh*
crab	蟹	*háaih*
crab apple	山楂	*sāan jā*
crabmeat	蟹肉	*háaih yuhk*
cracker	餅乾	*béng gōn*
cream	奶油	*náaih yàuh*
cream, whipped	發泡奶油	*faat póu náaih yàuh*
cream cheese	芝士	*jī sí*
crucian carp	鯽魚	*jāak yú*
cucumber	青瓜	*chēng gwā*
cumin	茴茜	*yìhm sāi*
cured pork	鹹肉	*hàahm yuhk*
custard	蒸蛋	*jīng dáan*
dessert wine	飯後甜酒	*faahn hauh tìhm jáu*
duck	鴨肉	*ngaap yuhk*
dumpling	餃子	*gáau jí*
eel	鰻魚	*maahn yú*
egg	雞蛋	*gāi dáan*
eggs with Chinese chives	韭菜炒雞蛋	*gáu choi cháau gāi dáan*
eggs with cucumber	黃瓜炒雞蛋	*wòhng gwā cháau gāi dáan*
eggs with a mixture of chopped meat and vegetables	芙蓉蛋	*fùh yùhng dáan*
eggs with peeled freshwater shrimp	蝦仁炒蛋	*hā yàhn cháau dáan*

pickled egg	皮蛋 *pèih dáan*
steamed egg	蒸蛋 *jīng dáan*
egg yolk/white	蛋黃／蛋白 *dáan wóng/dáan baahk*
eggplant [aubergine]	矮瓜 *ngái gwā*
fig	無花果 *mòuh fā gwó*
fish	魚 *yú*
French fries	炸薯條 *ja syùh tíu*
fritter	油炸餡餅 *yàuh ja háam béng*
fruit	生果 *sāang gwó*
game	野味 *yéh méi*
garlic	蒜 *syun*
garlic sauce	蒜香汁 *syun hēung jāp*
gin	氈酒 *jīn jáu*
ginger	薑 *gēung*
goat	羊肉 *yèuhng yuhk*
goose	鵝肉 *ngòh yuhk*
gooseberry	鵝莓 *ngòh múi*
grapefruit	西柚 *sāi yáu*
grapes	提子 *tàih jí*
grass carp	草魚 *chóu yú*
green bean	青豆 *chēng dáu*

guava	石榴 *sehk láu*
haddock	黑線鱈 *hāk sin syut*
hake	無鬚鱈 *mòuh sōu syut*
halibut	大比目魚 *daaih béi muhk yú*
ham	火腿 *fó téui*
hamburger	漢堡包 *hon bóu bāau*
hazelnut	榛子 *jēun jí*
heart	心臟 *sām johng*
hen	母雞 *móuh gāi*
herring	鮋魚 *pàaih yú*
honey	蜂蜜 *fūng maht*
hot dog	熱狗 *yiht gáu*
hot pepper sauce	辣醬 *laaht jeung*
ice (cube)	冰 *bīng*
ice cream	雪糕 *syut gōu*
jam	果占 *gwó jīm*
jelly	啫厘 *jē léi*
juice	果汁 *gwó jāp*
ketchup	茄汁 *ké jāp*
kid (young goat)	小羊肉 *síu yèuhng yuhk*
kidney	腰 *yīu*
kiwi	奇異果 *kèih yih gwó*
lamb	羊肉 *yèuhng yuhk*
leg	大腿肉 *daaih téui yuhk*
lemon	檸檬 *nìhng mūng*
lemonade	檸檬水 *nìhng mūng séui*
lentil	扁豆 *bín dáu*
lettuce	生菜 *sāang choi*
lime	青檸 *chēng níng*
liver	肝 *gōn*
lobster	龍蝦 *lùhng hā*

longan fruit	龍眼	*lùhng ngáahn*
macaroni	通心粉	*tūng sām fán*
mackerel	鯖魚	*chīng yú*
mandarin orange	柑	*gām*
mango	芒果	*mōng gwó*
margarine	沙律醬	*sā léut jeung*
marzipan	小杏仁餅	*síu hahng yàhn béng*
mayonnaise	沙律醬	*sā léut jeung*
meat	肉	*yuhk*
melon	瓜	*gwā*
meringue	蛋白甜餅	*dáan baahk tìhm béng*
milk	牛奶	*ngàuh náaih*
milk shake	奶昔	*náaih sīk*
mint	薄荷	*bohk hòh*
monkfish	扁鯊	*bín sā*
mushroom	蘑菇	*mòh gū*
mussel	青口	*chēng háu*
mustard	芥辣	*gaai laaht*
mutton	羊肉	*yèuhng yuhk*
noodle	麵	*mihn*
nori (a type of seaweed)	紫菜	*jí choi*
nougat	牛奶糖	*ngàuh náaih tóng*
nutmeg	豆蔻	*dauh kau*
nuts	硬殼果	*ngaahng hok gwó*
octopus	章魚	*jēung yùh*
olive	橄欖	*gaam láam*
olive oil	橄欖油	*gaam láam yàuh*
omelet	菴列	*ngām liht*
onion	蔥	*chūng*
orange	橙	*cháang*

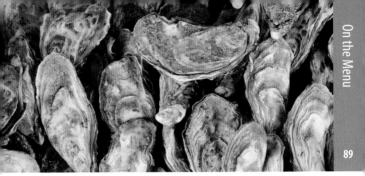

orange liqueur	甜橙酒 *tìhm cháang jáu*
organ meat [offal]	雜碎 *jaahp seui*
ox	黃牛肉 *wòhng ngàuh yuhk*
oxtail	牛尾 *ngàuh méih*
oyster	蠔 *hòuh*
pancake	薄煎餅 *bohk jīn béng*
papaya	木瓜 *muhk gwā*
paprika	辣椒粉 *laaht jiu fán*
pastry	酥皮點心 *sōu péi dím sām*
peach	桃 *tóu*
peanut	花生 *fā sāng*
pear	梨 *léi*
peas	豌豆 *wún dáu*
pecan	合桃 *hahp tòuh*
pepper (seasoning)	胡椒 *wùh jīu*
pepper (vegetable)	辣椒 *laaht jīu*
pheasant	野雞 *yéh gāi*
pickle	泡菜 *paau choi*
pie	餅 *béng*
pineapple	菠蘿 *bō lòh*
pizza	比薩 *pī sàh*

plum	李	*léih*
pomegranate	石榴	*sehk láu*
pork	豬肉	*jyū yuhk*
port	缽酒	*būt jáu*
potato	薯仔	*syùh jái*
potato chips [crisps]	薯片	*syùh pín*
prune	梅	*múi*
pumpkin	南瓜	*nàahm gwā*
quail	鵪鶉	*ngām chēun*
rabbit	兔仔肉	*tou jái yuhk*
radish	蘿蔔	*lòh baahk*
raisin	提子乾	*tàih jí gōn*
red bayberry	楊梅	*yèuhng múi*
red cabbage	紅葉椰菜	*hùhng yihp yèh choi*
relish	調味品	*tìuh meih bán*
rice	米	*máih*
roast	燒	*sīu*
roast beef	烤牛肉	*hāau ngàuh yuhk*
roll	卷	*gyún*
rum	林酒	*lām jáu*
salad	沙律	*sā léut*

salami	沙樂美腸	*sā lohk méih chéung*
salmon	三文魚	*sāam màhn yú*
salt	鹽	*yìhm*
sandwich	三文治	*sāam màhn jih*
sardine	沙甸魚	*sā dīn yú*
sauce	調味汁	*tìuh meih jāp*
sausage	香腸	*hēung chéung*
scallion [spring onion]	大蔥	*daaih syun*
scallop	扇貝	*sin bui*
scotch	蘇格蘭威士忌	*sōu gaak làahn wāi sih géi*
sea bass	鱸魚	*lòuh yú*
sea perch	中國花鱸	*jūng gwok fā lòuh*
seafood	海鮮	*hói sīn*
seaweed	海帶	*hói daai*
shallot	蔥	*chūng*
shank	小腿肉	*síu téui yuhk*
shellfish	貝類	*bui leuih*
sherry	些利酒	*sē leih jáu*
shrimp	蝦	*hā*
silver carp	鰱魚	*lìhn yú*
sirloin	牛腩	*ngàuh náahm*
snack	小食	*síu sihk*
snail	蝸牛	*wō ngàuh*
soda	蘇打水	*sō dá séui*
sole	板魚	*báan yú*
soup	湯	*tōng*
sour cream	酸奶油	*syūn náaih yàuh*
soy [soya]	大豆	*daaih dáu*
soy sauce	豉油	*sih yàuh*
soybean [soya bean]	大豆	*daaih dáu*
soymilk [soya milk]	豆奶	*dauh náaih*

spaghetti	意大利粉 *yi daaih leih fán*
spices	香料 *hēung líu*
spinach	菠菜 *bō choi*
spirits	酒 *jáu*
squash	南瓜 *nàahm gwā*
squid	烏賊 *wū chaak*
steak	牛扒 *ngàuh pá*
strawberry	士多啤厘 *sih dō bē léi*
suckling pig	乳豬 *yúh jyū*
sugar	糖 *tòhng*
sweet and sour sauce	甜酸醬 *tìhm syūn jeung*
sweet corn	粟米 *sūk mái*
sweet pepper	甜椒 *tìhm jīu*
sweet potato	番薯 *fāan syú*
sweetener	糖精 *tòhng jīng*
sweets	糖 *tóng*
swordfish	劍魚 *gim yú*
syrup	糖漿 *tòhng jēung*
tea	茶 *chàh*
thyme	麝香草 *seh hēung chóu*
tofu	豆腐 *dauh fuh*
breaded tofu	鍋塌豆腐 *wō taap dauh fuh*
cold tofu with garlic sauce	涼拌豆腐 *lèuhng buhn dauh fuh*
crushed tofu with pickled egg	皮蛋豆腐 *pèih dáan dauh fuh*
fried, stuffed tofu	鍋貼豆腐 *wō tip dauh fuh*
spicy tofu	麻婆豆腐 *màh pòh dauh fuh*
tofu in a clay pot	沙鍋豆腐 *sā wō dauh fuh*
tofu with fish	魚片豆腐 *yùh pín dauh fuh*

tofu with meatballs	肉丸豆腐 *yuhk yún dauh fuh*
tofu with peeled freshwater shimp	蝦仁豆腐 *hā yàhn dauh fuh*
toast	多士 *dō sí*
tomato	蕃茄 *fāan ké*
tongue	舌 *sit*
tripe	肚 *tóuh*
trout	鱒魚 *jēung yú*
truffles	菌 *kwán*
tuna	金槍魚 *gām chōng yú*
turkey	火雞 *fó gāi*
turnip	白蘿蔔 *baahk lòh baahk*
vanilla	雲尼拿 *wahn nēi ná*
veal	牛肉 *ngàuh yuhk*
vegetable	菜 *choi*
venison	鹿肉 *luhk yuhk*
vermouth	苦艾酒 *fú ngaaih jáu*
vinegar	醋 *chou*
vodka	伏特加 *fuhk dahk gā*
walnut	合桃 *hahp tòuh*

water	水 *séui*
watermelon	西瓜 *sāi gwā*
wheat	麵粉 *mihn fán*
whisky	威士忌 *wāi sih géi*
wine	葡萄酒 *pòuh tòuh jáu*
yogurt	乳酪 *yúh lohk*

People

Conversation

ESSENTIAL

Hello!	你好！ *néih hóu*
How are you?	你好嗎？ *néih hóu ma*
Fine, thanks.	好好，多謝。 *hóu hóu dō jeh*
Excuse me!	唔該！ *m gōi*
Do you speak English?	你講唔講英文？ *néih góng m góng yīng màhn*
What's your name?	你叫乜野名？ *néih giu māt yéh méng*
My name is...	我叫… *ngóh giu…*
Nice to meet you.	好高興見到你。 *hóu gōu hing gin dóu néih*
Where are you from?	你喺邊度嚟？ *néih hái bīn douh làih*
I'm from the U.S./U.K.	我喺美國/英國嚟。 *ngóh hái méih gwok/yīng gwok làih*
What do you do?	你做乜野工作？ *néih jouh māt yéh gūng jok*
I work for...	我喺…做野 *ngóh hái…jouh yéh*
I'm a student.	我係學生。 *ngóh haih hohk sāang*
I'm retired.	我退咗休。 *ngóh teui jó yāu*
Do you like...?	你想…？ *néih séung…*
Goodbye.	再見。 *joi gin*

It is polite to address people with: 先生 *sin sāang* (Sir), 女士 *néuih sih* (Madam) or 小姐 *síu jé* (Miss). The Chinese give special respect to older men and women by addressing them with 哥哥 *gòh gō* and 姐姐 *jèh jē*, respectively.

Language Difficulties

Do you speak English?	你講唔講英文？	*néih góng m góng yīng màhn*
Does anyone here speak English?	呢度邊個識講英文？	*nī douh bīn go sīk góng yīng màhn*
I don't speak Chinese.	我唔識講中文。	*ngóh m sīk góng jūng màhn*
Can you speak more slowly?	你可唔可以講慢啲？	*néih hó m hó yíh góng maahn dī*
Can you repeat that?	你可唔可以再講一次？	*néih hó m hó yíh joi góng yāt chi*
Excuse me?	唔該？	*m gōi*
What was that?	呢個係乜野？	*nī go haih māt yéh*
Can you spell it?	你可唔可以串出嚟？	*néih hó m hó yíh chyun chēut làih*
Please write it down.	唔該你寫低。	*m gōi néih sé dāi*
Can you translate this into English for me?	你可唔可以將呢個翻譯成英文？	*néih hó m hó yíh jēung nī go fāan yihk sìhng yīng màhn*
What does this/ that mean?	呢個/嗰個係乜野意思？	*nī go/gó go haih māt yéh yi sī*
I understand.	我明白喇。	*ngóh mìhng baahk la*

| I don't understand. | 我唔明白。 *ngóh m mìhng baahk* |
| Do you understand? | 你明白未？ *néih mìhng baahk meih* |

YOU MAY HEAR...

| 我講少少英文。 *ngóh góng síu síu yīng màhn* | I only speak a little English. |
| 我唔識講英文。 *ngóh m sīk góng yīng màhn* | I don't speak English. |

Making Friends

Hello!	你好！ *néih hóu*
Good morning.	早晨。 *jóu sàhn*
My name is...	我嘅名係… *ngóh ge méng haih…*
What's your name?	你叫乜野名？ *néih giu māt yéh méng*
I'd like to introduce you to...	我想同你介紹… *ngóh séung tùhng néih gaai siuh…*
Pleased to meet you.	好高興見到你。 *hóu gōu hing gin dóu néih*

A light, quick handshake is generally an accepted greeting in
China. A subtle nod and slight bow are other common greetings.
You may also see a person lowering his or her eyes upon meeting
someone; this is a gesture of respect.

How are you?	你好嗎?	*néih hóu ma*
Fine, thanks. And you?	好好，多謝。 你呢？	*hóu hóu dō jeh néih nē*

Travel Talk

I'm here…	我喺呢度…	*ngóh hái nī douh…*
on business	工幹	*gūng gon*
on vacation [holiday]	度假	*douh ga*
studying	讀書	*duhk syū*
I'm staying for…	我要留…	*ngóh yiu làuh…*
I've been here…	我喺呢度已經…喇	*ngóh hái nī douh yíh gīng…la*
a day	一日	*yāt yaht*
a week	一個星期	*yāt go sīng kèih*
a month	一個月	*yāt go yuht*
Where are you from?	你喺邊度嚟?	*néih hái bīn douh làih*
I'm from…	我喺…嚟。	*ngóh hái…làih*

For Numbers, see page 160.

Personal

Who are you with?	你同邊個一齊嚟？	*néih tùhng bīn go yāt chàih lài*
I'm here alone.	我一個人嚟嘅。	*ngóh yāt go yàhn lài*
I'm with my...	我同我嘅…一齊嚟嘅。	*ngóh tùhng ngóh ge... yāt chàih lài ge*
husband/wife	老公/老婆	*lóu gūng/lóuh pòh*
boyfriend/girlfriend	男/女朋友	*nàahm/néuih pàhng yáuh*
friend/colleague	朋友/同事	*pàhng yáuh/tùhng sih*
When's your birthday?	你嘅生日係幾時？	*néih ge sāang yaht haih géi sìh*
How old are you?	你幾大年紀？	*néih géi daaih nìhn géi*
I'm...	我…	*ngóh...*
Are you married?	你結咗婚未？	*néih git jó fān meih a*
I'm...	我…	*ngóh...*
single/in a relationship	單身/有固定朋友	*dāan sān/yáuh gu dihng pàhng yáuh*
engaged/married	訂咗婚/結咗婚	*dihng jó fān/git jó fān*
divorced/separated	離咗婚/分咗居	*lèih jó fān/fān jó gēui*
widowed	老公 **m**/老婆 **f** 過咗身	*lóuh gūng / lóuh pòh gwo jó sān*
Do you have children/ grandchildren?	你有冇細蚊仔/孫仔？	*néih yáuh móuh sai mān jái/syūn jái*

For Numbers, see page 160.

Work & School

What do you do?	你做乜野工作？	*néih jouh māt yéh gūng jok*
What are you studying?	你學緊乜野？	*néih hohk gán māt yéh*
I'm studying Chinese.	我學緊中文。	*ngóh hohk gán jūng màhn*

I…	我… ngóh…
am a consultant	係一個顧問 haih yāt go gu mahn
work full-time/ part-time	全職工作/兼職工作 chyùhn jīk gūng jok/gīm jīk gūng jok
am unemployed	失咗業 sāt jó yihp
work at home	喺屋企工作 hái ngūk kéi gūng jok
Who do you work for?	你幫邊個工作？ néih bōng bīn go gūng jok
I work for…	我幫…工作。 ngóh bōng…gūng jok
Here's my business card.	呢張係我嘅咭片。 nī jēung haih ngóh ge kāat pín

For Business Travel, see page 136.

Weather

What's the forecast?	天氣預告點？ tīn hei yuh gou dím
What beautiful/ terrible weather!	今日天氣真係好/唔好！ gām yaht tīn hei jān haih hóu/m̀ hóu
It's…	今日… gām yaht…
cool/warm	涼/暖 lèuhng/nyúhn
cold/hot	凍/熱 dung/yiht
rainy/sunny	落雨/好天 lohk yúh/hóu tīn
snowy/icy	落雪/有冰 lohk syut/yáuh bīng
Do I need a jacket/ an umbrella?	我需唔需要外套/遮？ ngóh sēui m̀ sēui yiu ngoih tou/jē

For Temperature, see page 167.

Romance

ESSENTIAL

Would you like to go out for a drink/ dinner?	你想唔想出去飲野/食晚飯？ *néih séung m séung chēut heui yám yéh/ sihk máahn faahn*
What are your plans for tonight/ tomorrow?	今晚/聽日你有乜野計畫？ *gām máahn/ tīng yaht néih yáuh māt yéh gai waahk*
Can I have your number?	可唔可以畀你嘅電話號碼我？ *hó m hó yíh béi néih ge dihn wá houh máh ngóh*
Can I join you?	我可唔可以加入？ *ngóh hó m hó yíh g ā yahp*
Can I get you a drink?	我可唔可以請你飲野？ *ngóh hó m hó yíh chéng néih yám yéh*
I like/love you.	我鍾意/愛你。 *ngóh jūng yi/ngoi néih*

102

The Dating Game

Would you like to go out for coffee?	你想唔想出去飲咖啡？ *néih séung m séung ch ēut heui yám ga fē*
Would you like to go out...?	你想唔想出去…? *néih séung m séung chēut heui*
for a drink	飲杯嘢 *yám būi yéh*
for dinner	食飯？ *sihk faahn*
What are your plans for...?	你…有乜野計畫？ *néih…yáuh māt yéh gai waahk*
today	今日 *gām yaht*
tonight	今晚 *gām máahn*
tomorrow	聽日 *tīng yaht*
this weekend	呢個週末 *nī go jāu muht*

Where would you like to go?	你想去邊度？ *néih séung heui bīn douh*
I'd like to go to…	我想去… *ngóh séung heui…*
Do you like…?	你鍾唔鍾意…？ *néih jūng m jūng yi…*
Can I have your number/e-mail?	可唔可以畀你嘅電話號碼/電郵我？ *hó m hó yíh béi néih ge dihn wá houh máh/dihn yàuh ngóh*
Are you on Facebook/Twitter?	你有冇註冊Facebook/Twitter？ *néih yáuh móuh jyu chaak Facebook/Twitter*
Can I join you?	我可唔可以加入？ *ngóh hó m hó yíh gā yahp*
You're very attractive.	你非常靚。 *néih fēi sèuhng leng*
Let's go somewhere quieter.	我哋去個安靜啲嘅地方啦。 *ngóh deih heui go ngōn jihng dī ge deih fōng lā*

Accepting & Rejecting

OK.	好。 *hóu*
Where should we meet?	我哋喺邊度見面？ *ngóh deih hái bīn douh gin mihn*
I'll meet you at the bar/at your hotel.	我喺酒吧/你嘅酒店見你。 *ngóh hái jáu bī/néih ge jáu dim gin néih*
I'll come by at…	我…探你。 *ngóh…taam néih*
What is your address?	你嘅地址係乜野？ *néih ge deih jí haih māt yéh*
Can we make it earlier/later?	我哋可唔可以早/夜啲？ *ngóh deih hó m hó yíh jóu/yeh dī*
How about another time?	第二個時間好唔好？ *daih yih go sìh gaan hóu m hóu*
I'm busy.	我好忙。 *ngóh hóu mòhng*
I'm not interested.	我冇興趣。 *ngóh móuh hing cheui*
Leave me alone.	我一個人得喇。 *ngóh yāt go yàhn dāk la*
Stop bothering me!	唔使理我！ *m sái léih ngóh*

The Chinese are generally reserved and may not be comfortable when asked forward questions regarding romance or sexuality.

Getting Intimate

Can I hug/kiss you?	我可唔可以攬住/錫你?	*ngóh hó m hó yíh láam jyuh/sek néih*
Yes.	得。	*dāk*
No.	唔得。	*m dāk*
I like/love you.	我鍾意/愛你。	*ngóh jūng yi/ngoih néih*
Stop!	停!	*tìhng*

Sexual Preferences

Are you gay?	你係唔係男同性戀者?	*néih haih m haih nàahm tùhng sing lyún jé*
I'm...	我係···	*ngóh haih...*
heterosexual	異性戀	*yih sing lyún*
homosexual	同性戀	*tùhng sing lyún*
bisexual	雙性戀者	*sēung sing lyún jé*
Do you like men/ women?	你鍾唔鍾意男人/女人?	*néih jūng m jūng yi nàahm yán/néuih yán*
Let's go to a gay bar.	我哋去一間基吧啦	*ngóh deih heui yāt gāan gēi bā lā*

Chinese attitudes regarding homosexuality are conservative; therefore, asking about a person's sexuality may not be an appropriate question. Drawing attention to one's sexual orientation is generally discouraged. The gay community in major Chinese cities is growing, though. Larger cities in China may have gay-friendly bars and clubs but often in discreet locations.

Leisure Time

Sightseeing

ESSENTIAL

Where's the tourist information office?	旅遊資訊辦公室喺邊度？	*léuih yàuh jī seun baahn gūng sāt hái bīn douh*
What are the main attractions?	主要景點係乜野？	*jyú yiu gíng dím haih māt yéh*
Do you have tours in English?	有冇英文導遊？	*yáuh móuh yīng màhn douh yàuh*
Can I have a map/ guide?	我可唔可以要一張地圖/旅遊指南？	*ngóh hó m hó yíh yiu yāt jēung deih tòuh/léuih yàuh jí nàahm*

Tourist Information

Do you have information on…?	你有冇⋯嘅資訊？	*néih yáuh móuh…ge jī seun*
How do we get there?	我哋點去嗰度？	*ngóh deih dím heui gó douh*
Can you recommend…?	你可唔可以介紹⋯？	*néih hó m hó yíh gaai siuh…*
a bus tour	巴士遊覽	*bā sí yàuh láahm*
an excursion to…	去⋯遊覽	*heui…yàuh láahm*
a sightseeing tour	觀光遊覽	*gūn gwōng yàuh láahm*

On Tour

I'd like to go on the tour to…	我想去⋯遊覽。	*ngóh séung heui…yàuh láahm*
When's the next tour?	下一團幾時？	*hah yāt tyùhn géi sìh*

Travel agencies that often cater to foreigners include China
Travel Services (www.chinatravelservice.com) and China
International Travel Service (www.cits.net); the latter has branches
throughout China. Such agencies offer a variety of services (these vary
by location) such as arranging tours; reserving places to stay; providing
tickets for trains, operas, acrobatic performances, concerts and more.
Small-scale tour operators can also be of assistance; be sure that the
tour operator is licensed before requesting any service.

Are there tours in English?	有冇英文導遊？	*yáuh móuh yīng màhn douh yàuh*
Is there an English guide book/audio guide?	有冇英文嘅旅遊手冊／錄音旅遊指南？	*yáuh móuh yīng màhn ge léuih yàuh sáu chaak/luhk yām léuih yàuh jí nàahm*
What time do we leave/return?	我哋幾時出發／返嚟？	*ngóh deih géi sìh chēut faat/fāan làih*
We'd like to see...	我哋想睇睇⋯	*ngóh deih séung tái tái...*
Can we stop here...?	我哋可唔可以停喺呢度⋯？	*ngóh deih hó m hó yíh tìhng hái nī douh...*
to take photos	影相	*yíng séung*
for souvenirs	買紀念品	*máaih gei nihm bán*
for the restrooms [toilets]	去洗手間	*heui sái sáu gāan*
Is it disabled-accessible?	殘疾人可唔可以用？	*chàahn jiht yàhn hó m hó yíh yuhng*

For Tickets, see page 21.

Seeing the Sights

Where is/are…?	…喺邊度？	…hái bīn douh
the battleground	戰場	jin chèuhng
the botanical garden	植物公園	jihk maht gūng yún
Where is/are…?	…喺邊度？	…hái bīn douh
the castle	城堡	sèhng bóu
city hall	市政大廳	síh jing daaih tēng
the downtown area	市中心	síh jūng sām
the fountain	噴水池	pan séui chìh
the city hall	大會堂	daaih wuih tòhng
the library	圖書館	tòuh syū gún
the market	商場	sēung chèuhng
the (war) memorial	（戰爭）紀念館	(jin jāng) gei nihm gún
the museum	博物館	bohk maht gún
the old town	古鎮	gú jan
the opera house	歌劇院	gō kehk yún
the palace	宮殿	gūng dihn
the park	公園	gūng yún
the ruins	遺跡	wàih jīk
the shopping area	購物區	kau maht kēui

Can you show me on the map?	你可唔可以喺地圖上面指畀我睇？ *néih hó m hó yíh hái deih tòuh seuhng mihn jí béi ngóh tái*
Is it disabled accessible?	殘疾人可唔可以用？ *chàahn jaht yàhn hó m hó yíh yuhng*
It's...	好 ⋯ *hóu...*
amazing	犀利 *sāi leih*
beautiful	靚 *leng*
boring	悶 *muhn*
interesting	有意思 *yáuh yi sī*
magnificent	壯觀 *jong gūn*
romantic	浪漫 *lohng maahn*
strange	奇怪 *kèih gwaai*
stunning	令人震驚 *lihng yàhn jan gīng*
terrible	可怕 *hó pa*
ugly	難睇 *nàahn tái*
I (don't) like it.	我（唔）鍾意。 *ngóh (m) jūng yi*

For Asking Directions, see page 36.

Sights in China not to be missed include: the Great Wall, Imperial Palace, Summer Palace, Temple of Heaven, Ming tombs and Xi'an terracotta warriors. Temples, gardens and other sights can be found in even the smallest towns. For local sights, check with your hotel concierge or a nearby travel agency. Sights are listed on town maps, which can be purchased at newsstands and from street vendors. There is so much to see in China.

In the evenings, entertainment such as concerts, acrobatics, Chinese ballet and opera are available. Of these, a not-to-be-missed event is the Canton opera, a spectacular combination of song, dance, pantomime and martial arts.

Religious Sites

Where's…?	…喺邊度？	…hái bīn douh
the Catholic/	天主教/新教徒教堂	tīn jyú gaau/sān gaau
Protestant church		tòuh gaau tóng
the mosque	清真寺	chīng jān jí
the shrine	神殿	sàhn dihn
the synagogue	猶太教堂	yàuh taai gaau tòhng
the temple	寺廟	jih míu
What time is mass/	彌撒/禮拜係幾時？	nèih saat/láih baai haih
the service?		géi sìh

The People's Republic of China officially subscribes to atheism but, since China's reform, open religious activity has been permitted. Buddhism is the most widely practiced religion in China. Taoism, Islam and Christianity are also observed.

Religion in Hong Kong and Macau is not suppressed. You can find churches and temples in the main cities.

Shopping

ESSENTIAL

Where's the market/ mall [shopping centre]?	街市/購物中心喺邊度？	*gāai síh/kau maht jūng sām hái bīn douh*
I'm just looking.	我淨係睇吓。	*ngóh jihng haih tái háh*
Can you help me?	你可唔可以幫我？	*néih hó m hó yíh bōng ngóh*
I'm being helped.	有人幫我喇。	*yáuh yàhn bōng ngóh la*
How much?	幾多錢？	*géi dō chín*
That one, please.	唔該畀嗰個我。	*m gōi béi gó go ngóh*
That's all.	就呢啲。	*jauh nī dī*
Where can I pay?	我喺邊度畀錢？	*ngóh hái bīn douh béi chín*
I'll pay in cash/by credit card.	我用現金/信用卡畀錢。	*ngóh yuhng yihn gām/seun yuhng kāat béi chín*
A receipt, please.	唔該畀收據我。	*m gōi béi sāu geui ngóh*

At the Shops

Where's…?	…喺邊度？	…hái bīn douh
the antiques store	古董店	gú dúng dim
the bakery	麵包舖	mihn bāau póu
the bank	銀行	ngàhn hòhng
the bookstore	書店	syū dim
the camera store	相機舖	séung gēi póu
the clothing store	時裝店	sìh jōng dim
the delicatessen	熟食店	suhk sihk dim
the department store	百貨公司	baak fo gūng sī
the gift shop	禮品店	láih bán dim
the health food store	健康食品店	gihn hōng sihk bán dim
the jeweler	珠寶店	jyū bóu dim
the liquor store [off-licence]	洋酒店	yèuhng jáu dim
the mall [shopping centre]	購物中心	kau maht jūng sām
the market	街市	gāai síh
the music store	音樂商店	yām ngohk sēung dim
Where's…?	…喺邊度？	…hái bīn douh
the pastry shop	麵包點心店	mihn bāau dím sām dim
the pharmacy	藥房	yeuhk fòhng
the produce [grocery] store	食品店	sihk bán dim

Department stores often sell quality goods produced for export and offer a nice selection of souvenirs. Some department stores can send purchases abroad.

YOU MAY HEAR...

我可唔可以幫你？ *ngóh hó m hó yíh bōng néih*

Can I help you?

唔該等一等。 *m gōi dáng yāt dáng*

One moment.

你要乜野？ *néih yiu māt yéh*

What would you like?

仲要唔要第二啲？ *juhng yiu m yiu daih yih dī*

Anything else?

the shoe store	鞋鋪	*hàaih póu*
the souvenir store	紀念品商店	*gei nihm bán sēung dim*
the supermarket	超級市場	*chīu kāp síh chèuhng*
the tobacconist	煙草鋪	*yīn chóu pou*
the toy store	玩具鋪	*wuhn geuih póu*

Ask an Assistant

When do you open/close?	幾點開門/閂門？	*géi dím hōi mùhn/sāan mùhn*
Where's...?	…喺邊度？	*...hái bīn douh*
the cashier	收銀處	*sāu ngán chyu*
the escalator	電梯	*dihn tāi*
the elevator [lift]	電梯	*dihn tāi*
the fitting room	試身室	*si sān sāt*
the store directory	士多目錄	*sih dō muhk luhk*
Can you help me?	你可唔可以幫我？	*néih hó m hó yíh bōng ngóh*
I'm just looking.	我只係睇睇。	*ngóh jí haih tái tái*
I'm being helped.	已經有人幫我喇。	*yíh gīng yáuh yàhn bōng ngóh la*
Do you have...?	你有冇…？	*néih yáuh móuh...*
Can you show me...?	你可唔可以畀…我睇睇？	*néih hó m hó yíh béi...ngóh tái tái*

Can you ship/ wrap it?	你可唔可以將呢啲野托運/打包？ *nèih hó m hó yíh jēung nī dī yéh tok wahn/dá bāau*
How much?	幾多錢？ *géi dō chín*
That's all.	就呢啲。 *jauh nī dī*

YOU MAY SEE...

開門 *hōi mùhn*	open
閂門 *sāan mùhn*	closed
午飯時間關門 *ngh faahn sìh gaan gwāan mùhn*	closed for lunch
試身室 *sì sān sāt*	fitting room
付款處 *fuh fún chyu*	cashier
只收現金 *jí sāu yihn gām*	cash only
接受信用卡 *jip sauh seun yuhng kāat*	credit cards accepted
營業時間 *yìhng yihp sìh gaan*	business hours
出口 *chēut háu*	exit

Personal Preferences

I'd like something...	我想要… *ngóh séung yiu...*
cheap/expensive	平啲/貴啲嘅 *pèhng dī/gwai dī ge*
larger/smaller	大啲/細啲嘅 *daaih dī/sai dī ge*
nicer	好啲嘅 *hóu dī ge*
from this region	當地生產嘅 *dōng deih sāng cháan ge*
Around...HK dollars.	…蚊左右嘅。 *...mān jó yáu ge*
Is it real?	呢啲係唔係真嘅？ *nī dī haih m haih jān ge*
Can you show me this/that?	你可唔可以畀我睇吓呢個/嗰個？ *néih hó m hó yíh béi ngóh tái háh nī go/gó go*
That's not quite what I want.	嗰個唔係我要嘅。 *gó go m haih ngóh yiu ge*

No, I don't like it.	我唔鍾意。 *ngóh m jūng yi*
It's too expensive.	太貴喇。 *taai gwai la*
I have to think about it.	我要諗諗。 *ngóh yiu nám nám*
I'll take it.	我要。 *ngóh yiu*

Paying & Bargaining

How much?	幾多錢？ *géi dō chín*
I'll pay...	我要用…畀錢。 *ngóh yiu yuhng...béi chín*
in cash	現金 *yihn gām*
by credit card	信用卡 *seun yuhng kāat*
by traveler's check [cheque]	旅行支票 *léuih hàhng jī piu*
Can I use this...?	我可唔可以用…卡？ *ngóh hó m hó yíh yuhng...kāat*
ATM	自動提款機 *jih duhng tàih fún gēi*
credit	信用 *seun yuhng*
gift	禮品 *láih bán*
How do I use this machine?	呢架機器點樣用？ *nī ga gēi hei dím yéung yuhng*
A receipt, please.	唔該畀收據我。 *m gōi béi sāu geui ngóh*
That's too much.	太貴喇。 *taai gwai la*
I'll give you...	我畀…你。 *ngóh béi...néih*
I have only...Hong Kong dollars.	我只有…港幣。 *ngóh jí yáuh...góng baih*

In Hong Kong and throughout China, the most commonly accepted form of payment is cash. Major credit cards may be accepted at larger stores in city centers.

YOU MAY HEAR...

你點樣畀錢？ *néih dím yéung béi chín* — How are you paying?

你嘅信用卡被拒絕。 — Your credit card has been declined.
néih ge seun yuhng kāat beih kéuih jyuht

唔該出示你嘅身份證。 — ID, please.
m gōi chēut sih néih ge sān fán jing

我哋唔接受信用卡。 — We don't accept credit cards.
ngóh deih m jip sauh seun yuhng kāat

唔該畀現金。 *m gōi béi yihn gām* — Cash only, please.

Is that your best price?	係唔係最低價？	*haih m haih jeui dāi ga*
Can you give me a discount?	可唔可以打折？	*hó m hó yíh dá jit*

Making a Complaint

I'd like...	我想… *ngóh séung…*
to exchange this	換一個 *wuhn yāt go*
a refund	退款 *teui fún*
to see the manager	見經理 *gin gīng léih*

Services

Can you recommend...?	你可唔可以介紹…？ *néih hó m hó yíh gaai siuh…*
a barber	一位理髮師 *yāt wái léih faat sī*
a dry cleaner	一間乾洗店 *yāt gāan gōn sái dim*
a hairstylist	一位髮型師 *yāt wái faat yìhng sī*
a laundromat [launderette]	一間洗衣鋪 *yāt gāan sái yī póu*

a spa	一間溫泉 yāt gāan wān chyùhn
a travel agency	一間旅行社 yāt gāan léui hàhng séh
Can you...this?	你可唔可以…呢個？ néih hó m hó yíh… nī go
alter	改 gói
clean	洗 sái
fix [mend]	整 jíng
press	熨 tong
When will it be ready?	幾時做完？ géi sìh jouh yùhn

Hair & Beauty

I'd like...	我想… ngóh séung…
an appointment for today/ tomorrow	約一個今日/聽日嘅時間 yeuk yāt go gām yaht/tī ng yaht ge sìh gaan
some color/ highlights	染髮/挑染 yíhm faat/tīu yíhm
my hair blow-dried	吹頭 chēui tàuh
a haircut	剪頭髮 jín tàuh faat
a trim	剪髮 jín faat
Not too short.	唔好太短。 m hóu taai dyún
Shorter here.	呢度再短一啲。 nī douh joi dyún yāt dī
I'd like...	我想… ngóh séung…
a facial	做面部美容 jouh mihn bouh méih yùhng
a manicure/ pedicure	修手甲/腳甲 sāu sáu gaap/geuk gaap
a massage	要按摩 yiu ngon mō
Do you do...?	你做唔做…？ néih jouh m jouh…
acupuncture	針灸 jām gau
aromatherapy	香薰療法 hēung fān lìuh faat

A number of luxury hotels in China offer facial and body treatments and massage. Some even have unique amenities for spa guests, such as tea centers, Tai Chi and yoga lessons. Check with your hotel concierge or a travel agency for a list of spas, services and prices.

| oxygen treatment | 氧氣治療 *yéuhng hei jih lìuh* |
| Do you have a sauna? | 你做唔做桑拿？*néih jouh m jouh sōng nàh* |

Antiques

How old is it?	有幾長歷史？*yáuh géi chèuhng lihk sí*
Do you have anything from the...period?	你有冇···時期嘅野？*néih yáuh móuh...sìh kèih ge yéh*
Do I have to fill out any forms?	我使唔使填表？*ngóh sái m sái tìhn bíu*
Is there a certificate of authenticity?	有冇真品證明？*yáuh móuh jān bán jing mìhng*
Can you ship/wrap it?	你可唔可以送貨/包咗佢？*néih hó mhó yíh sung fo/ bāau jó kéuih*

Clothing

I'd like...	我想要··· *ngóh séung yiu...*
Can I try this on?	我可唔可以試著 *ngóh hó m hó yíh si jeuk*
It doesn't fit.	唔適合。*m sīk hahp*
It's too...	太··· *taai...*
big/small	大/細 *daaih/sai*
short/long	短/長 *dyún/chèuhng*
tight/loose	緊/闊 *gán/fut*
Do you have this in size...?	呢件衫有冇···號嘅？*nī gihn sāam yáuh móuh...houh ge*

Do you have this in a bigger/smaller size?	呢件衫有冇大/細啲嘅吗？ *nī gihn sāam yáuh móuh daaih/sai dī ge*

Colors

I'd like something...	我想要… *ngóh séung yiu…*
beige	米黃 *máih wòhng*
black	黑色 *hāak sīk*
blue	藍色 *làahm sīk*
brown	咖啡色 *ga fē sīk*
gray	灰色 *fūi sīk*
green	綠色 *luhk sīk*
orange	橙色 *cháang sīk*
pink	粉紅色 *fán hùhng sīk*

YOU MAY HEAR...

嗰件衫好適合你。 *nī gihn sāam hóu sīk hahp néih*	That looks great on you.
適唔適合我？ *sīk m sīk hahp ngóh*	How does it fit?
我哋冇你嘅尺寸。 *ngóh deih móuh néih ge chek chyun*	We don't have your size.

purple	紫色 *jí sīk*
red	紅色 *hùhng sīk*
white	白色 *baahk sīk*
yellow	黃色 *wòhng sīk*

Clothes & Accessories

backpack	背囊 *bui nòhng*
belt	皮帶 *pèih dáai*
bikini	比基尼 *béi gīn nèih*
blouse	女裝恤衫 *néuih jōng sēut sāam*
bra	胸圍 *hūng wàih*
briefs [underpants]/	男裝底褲／女裝底褲 *nàahm jōng dái fu/néuih*
panties	*jōng dái fu*
coat	外套 *ngoih tou*
dress	禮服 *láih fuhk*
hat	帽 *móu*
jacket	褸 *lāu*
jeans	牛仔褲 *ngàuh jái fu*
pajamas	睡衣 *seuih yī*
pants [trousers]	長褲 *chèuhng fu*
pantyhose [tights]	絲襪 *sī maht*
purse [handbag]	女裝銀包 *néuih jōng ngàhn bāau*
raincoat	雨褸 *yúh lāu*
scarf	絲巾 *sī gān*
shirt	恤衫 *sēut sām*
shorts	短褲 *dyún fu*
skirt	裙 *kwàhn*
socks	襪 *maht*
suit	套裝 *tou jōng*
sunglasses	太陽眼鏡 *taai yèuhng ngáhn géng*
sweater	毛衫 *mòuh sāam*

YOU MAY SEE...

男士嘅 *nàahm sih ge*		men's
女士嘅 *néuih sih ge*		women's
細蚊仔嘅 *sai mān jái ge*		children's

sweatshirt	運動衫 *wahn duhng sāam*
swimsuit	泳衣 *wihng yī*
T-shirt	T恤 *tī sēut*
tie	領呔 *léhng tāai*
underwear	底衫 *dái sāam*

Fabric

I'd like...	我想要··· *ngóh séung yiu...*
cotton	棉布 *mìhn bou*
denim	粗棉布 *chōu mìhn bou*
I'd like...	我想要··· *ngóh séung yiu...*
lace	花邊 *fā bīn*
leather	皮 *péi*
linen	麻布 *màh bou*
silk	絲綢 *sī chàuh*
wool	羊毛 *yèuhng mòuh*
Is it machine washable?	可唔可以機洗？ *hó m hó yíh gēi sái*

Western and traditional Chinese clothing is sold at street markets and local department stores, usually at very reasonable prices. Designer clothing is available at high-end boutiques, found in larger cities. China is known for its silk production, and silk clothing and fabric (sold by the yard) can be purchased in many stores.

In department stores and places where clothes are made for export, sizes will be given as small, medium and large. Most other clothing stores feature Chinese measurements that combine height and chest size; these measurements appear in centimeters. For example, if you are 170 cm tall (5'6") with a chest measurement of 90 cm (36"), look for clothing marked 170/90. Children's sizes are given by height, in centimeters.

Shoes

I'd like…	我想要··· *ngóh séung yiu…*
high-heels/flats	高掙鞋／平底鞋 *gōu jāang hàaih/pìhng dái hàaih*
boots	靴 *hēu*
loafers	平底便服鞋 *pìhng dái bihn fuhk hàaih*
sandals	涼鞋 *lèuhng hàaih*
shoes	鞋 *hàaih*
slippers	拖鞋 *tō háai*
sneakers	運動鞋 *wahn duhng hàaih*
In size…	···號 *…houh*

Sizes

chest measurement	胸圍 *hūng wàih*
waist measurement	腰圍 *yīu wàih*
height	身長 *sān chèuhng*
extra small (XS)	加細碼 *gā sai máh*
small (S)	細碼 *sai máh*
medium (M)	中碼 *jūng máh*
large (L)	大碼 *daaih máh*
extra large (XL)	加大碼 *gā daaih máh*
plus size	加加大碼 *gā gā daaih máh*

Newsagent & Tobacconist

Do you sell English-language newspapers?	你賣唔賣英文報紙？	néih maaih m maaih yīng màhn bou jí
I'd like...	我想買…	ngóh séung máaih...
candy [sweets]	糖 (甜品)	tóng (tìhm bán)
chewing-gum	香口膠	hēung háu gāau
a chocolate bar	朱古力	jyū gú lihk
a cigar	雪茄	syut kā
a pack/carton of cigarettes	一包/一條煙	yāt bāau/yāt tìuh yīn
a lighter	一個打火機	yāt go dá fó gēi
I'd like...	我想買…	ngóh séung máaih...
a magazine	一本雜誌	yāt bún jaahp ji
matches	火柴	fó chàaih
a newspaper	一份報紙	yāt fahn bou jí
a pen	一支筆	yāt jī bāt
a phone card	一張電話卡	yāt jēung dihn wá kāat
a postcard	一張明信片	yāt jēung mìhn seun pín
a road/town map of...	…道路/市區地圖	...douh louh/síh kēui deih tòuh
stamps	郵票	yàuh piu

123

China Daily is China's official English-language newspaper, available in most major cities. *South China Morning Post* is a popular English newspaper sold in Hong Kong and can be found in hotels and convenience stores. In larger cities, English-language and international magazines and newspapers are generally available at hotels and major newsstands. You may also find an English-language channel on your hotel TV.

Photography

I'd like…camera.	我想買一個…相機。	*ngóh séung máaih yāt go…séung gēi*
an automatic	自動	*jih duhng*
a digital	數碼	*sou máh*
a disposable	即棄	*jīk hei*
I'd like…	我想…	*ngóh séung…*
a battery	買一個電芯	*máaih yāt go dihn sām*
digital prints	數碼列印照片	*sou máh liht yan jiu pín*
a memory card	買存儲卡	*máaih chyúh jihk kaat*
Can I print digital photos here?	我可唔可以喺呢度列印數碼照片？	*ngóh hó m hó yíh hái nī douh liht yan sou máh jiu pín*

Souvenirs

book	書	*syū*
box of chocolates	朱古力	*jyū gū līk*
calligraphy supplies	書法用品	*syū faat yuhng bán*
Chinese painting	中國畫	*jūng gwok wá*
chopsticks	筷子	*faai jí*
cloisonné	景泰藍	*gíng taai làahm*
doll	公仔	*gūng jái*
jade	玉	*yúk*
key ring	鑰匙扣	*só sìh kau*
lacquerware	漆器	*chāt hei*
porcelain	瓷器	*chìh hei*
postcard	明信片	*mìhng seun pín*
pottery	瓷器	*chìh hei*
silk	絲綢	*sī chàuh*
T-shirt	T恤	*tī sēut*
toy	玩具	*wuhn geuih*
Can I see this/that?	我可唔可以睇睇呢個/嗰個？	*ngóh hó m hó yíh tái tái nī go/gó go*

It's in the window/ display case.	喺櫥窗/陳列櫃裏面。	*hái chyùh chēung/chàhn liht gwaih léuih mihn*
I'd like…	我想要…	*ngóh séung yiu…*
a battery	一個電芯	*yāt go dihn sām*
a bracelet	一隻手扼	*yāt jek sáu ngáak*
a brooch	一個心口針	*yāt go sām háu jām*
a clock	一個鐘	*yāt go jūng*
earrings	一對耳環	*yāt deui yíh wáan*
a necklace	一條頸鏈	*yāt tiuh géng lín*
a ring	一隻戒指	*yāt jek gaai jí*
a watch	一個手錶	*yāt go sáu bīu*
I'd like…	我想要…嘅。	*ngóh séung yiu…ge*
copper	銅	*tùhng*
crystal	水晶	*séui jīng*
diamonds	鑽石	*jyun sehk*
white/yellow gold	白/黃金	*baahk/wòhng gām*
I'd like…	我想要…嘅。	*ngóh séung yiu…ge*
pearls	珍珠	*jān jyū*
platinum	鉑金	*baahk gām*

Typical Chinese souvenirs include silk fabric and clothing, jade, pearls and porcelain. Jade is traditionally worn for good luck, as a protection against illness and as an amulet for travelers. Pearls are also part of Chinese tradition and were worn by emperors and other nobility. Calligraphy supplies, kites, paper cuts and chopsticks are also popular mementos. Souvenirs can be found in malls, department stores and local street markets.

If you're antiquing, note that items dated earlier than 1795 may not be legally exported; any antique leaving China must be affixed with a small red seal, provided by the Cultural Relics Bureau.

sterling silver	純銀 *sèuhn ngán*
Is this real?	呢啲係唔係真嘅？ *nī dī haih m haih jān ge*
Can you engrave it?	你可唔可以喺上面刻字？ *néih hó m hó yíh hái seuhng mihn hāk jih*

Sport & Leisure

ESSENTIAL

When's the game?	幾時比賽？ *géi sìh béi choi*
Where's...?	…喺邊度？ *...hái bīn douh*
the beach	海灘 *hói tāan*
the park	公園 *gūng yún*
the pool	泳池 *wihng chìh*
Is it safe to swim here?	喺呢度游水安唔安全？ *hái nī douh yàuh séui ngōn m ngōn chyùhn*
Can I rent [hire] golf clubs?	可唔可以租棒球？ *hó m hó yíh jōu kàuh páahng*
How much per hour?	每個鍾頭幾多錢？ *múih go jūng tàuh géi dō chín*
How far is it to...?	去…有幾遠？ *heui...yáuh géi yúhn*
Show me on the map, please.	唔該喺地圖上面指畀我睇。 *m gōi hái deih tòuh seuhng mihn jí béi ngóh tái*

Watching Sport

When's...game/ match?	…比賽係幾時？ *...béi choi haih géi sìh*
the badminton	羽毛球 *yúh mòuh kàuh*
the baseball	棒球 *páahng kàuh*
the basketball	籃球 *làahm kàuh*
the boxing	拳擊 *kyùhn gīk*
the golf	高爾夫球 *gōu yíh fū kàuh*

Early risers will no doubt encounter people practicing Tai Chi (太極 *taai gihk*), a combination of martial arts and relaxation movements, in parks throughout China. Some also practice Qigong (氣功 *hei gūng*), breathing and movement exercises. If you are interested in joining, the crowd would welcome you.

Other sports enjoyed in China include badminton and ping-pong. Volleyball courts and swimming pools can be found throughout China. If you're looking for brain exercise instead of a body stretch, try Mahjong (麻雀 *màh jeuk*), a popular Chinese strategy game. Chinese chess and cards are common as well.

the martial arts	武術	*móuh seuht*
the ping-pong	乒乓波	*bīng bām bō*
the soccer [football]	足球	*jūk kàuh*
the tennis	網球	*móhng kàuh*
the volleyball	排球	*pàaih kàuh*
the wrestling	摔跤	*sēut gāau*
Who's playing?	邊個打緊波？	*bīn go dá gán bō*
Where's the racetrack/stadium?	跑馬場/體育場喺邊度？	*páau máh chèuhng/ wahn duhng chèuhng hái bīn douh*
Where can I place a bet?	我可以喺邊度落注？	*ngóh hó yíh haih bīn douh ohk jyu*

Playing Sport

Where is/are...?	...喺邊度？	*...hái bīn douh*
the golf course	高爾夫球場	*gōu yíh fū kàuh chèuhng*
the gym	健身房	*gihn sān fòhng*
the park	公園	*gūng yún*
the tennis courts	網球場	*móhng kàuh chèuhng*

How much per...?	每···幾多錢? *múih...géi dō chín*
day	日 *yaht*
hour	個鐘頭 *go jūng tàuh*
game	場比賽 *chèuhng béi choi*
round	輪比賽 *lèuhn béi choi*
Can I rent [hire]...?	我可唔可以租···? *ngóh hó m hó yíh jōu...*
clubs	球棒 *kàuh páahng*
equipment	設備 *chit beih*
a racket	一個球拍 *yāt go kàuh paak*

At the Beach/Pool

Where's the beach/pool?	海灘/泳池喺邊度? *hói tāan/wihng chìh hái bīn douh*
Is there...?	有冇···? *yáuh móuh...*
a kiddie pool	兒童泳池 *yìh tùhng wihng chìh*
an indoor/ outdoor pool	室内/室外游泳池 *sāt noih/sāt ngoih yàuh wihng chìh*
a lifeguard	救生員 *gau sāng yùhn*
Is it safe...?	···安唔安全? *...ngōn m ngōn chyùhn*
to swim	游水 *yàuh séui*
to dive	潛水 *chìhm séui*
for children	細蚊仔用 *sai mān jái yuhng*
I'd like to hire...	我想租··· *ngóh séung jōu...*
a deck chair	一張接椅 *yāt jēung jip yí*
diving equipment	一套潛水用具 *yāt tou chìhm séui yuhng geuih*
I'd like to hire...	我想租··· *ngóh séung jōu...*
a jet ski	一套噴氣式滑水板 *yāt gou pan hei sīk waaht séui báan*
a motorboat	一艘汽艇 *yāt sáu hei téng*
a rowboat	一隻艇仔 *yāt jek téng jái*

Public beaches can be found around Hong Kong and along China's east coast. The most popular beaches are often very crowded, so arrive early for a good spot.

snorkeling equipment	潛水設備	*chìhm séui chi beih*
a surfboard	一塊滑浪板	*yāt faai waaht lohng báan*
a towel	一條毛巾	*yāt tìuh mòuh gān*
an umbrella	一把遮	*yāt bá jē*
water skis	滑水橇	*waaht séui hīu*
a windsurfer	一隻帆船	*yāt jek fàahn syùhn*
For…hours.	一共⋯個鐘頭。	*yāt guhng…go jūng tàuh*

Winter Sports

A ticket for the skating rink, please.	唔該一張溜冰場入場券。	*m gōi yāt jēung làuh bīng chèuhng yahp chèuhng hyun*
I want to rent [hire] ice skates.	我想租溜冰鞋。	*ngóh séung jòu làuh bīng hàaih*
Can I take skating lessons?	我可唔可以上溜冰堂	*ngóh hó m hó yíh séung làuh bīg tòhng*
I'm a beginner.	我係初學者。	*ngóh haih chō hohk jé*
A lift pass for a day/ five days, please.	一日／五日纜車接送，唔 該。	*yāt yaht/ńgh yaht laahm chē jip sung, m gōi*

Due to warm temperatures year-round, winter sports are generally not popular in Cantonese-speaking China. Skating rinks can be found inside some large shopping malls in Hong Kong.

YOU MAY SEE...

電梯 *dihn tāi*	lifts
牽引電梯 *hīn yáhn dihn tāi*	drag lift
纜車 *laahm chē*	cable car
升降椅 *sīng gong yí*	chair lift
新手 *sān sáu*	novice
中等水平 *jūng dáng séui pìhng*	intermediate
專家 *jyūn gā*	expert
小路 [滑雪道] 關咗 *síu louh [waaht syut douh] gwāan jó*	trail [piste] closed

I'd like to hire...	我想租···	*ngóh séung jōu*
boots	靴	*hēu*
a helmet	一個頭盔	*yāt go tàuh kwāi*
poles	雪杖	*syut jeuhng*
skis	滑雪板	*waaht syut bán*
a snowboard	一塊滑雪單板	*yāt faai waaht syut dāan báan*
snowshoes	雪地鞋	*yāt faai waaht syut dāan báan*
These are too big/small.	呢啲太大/太細	*nī dī taai daaih / taai sai*
Are there lessons?	有冇培訓課程?	*yáuh móuh pùih fan fo chìhng*
I'm experienced.	我有經驗。	*ngóh yáuh gīng yihm*
A trail map, please.	一幅地形圖，唔該。	*yāt fūk deih yìhng tòuh, m gōi*

Out in the Country

A map of..., please.	唔該畀一份···地圖我。	*m gōi béi yāt fahn... deih tòuh ngóh*
this region	呢個地區嘅	*nī go deih kēui ge*
the walking routes	步行路線	*bouh hàhng louh sin*

the bike routes	單車路線	*dāan chē louh sin*
the trails	行山道	*hàahng sāan douh*
Is it…?	係唔係…?	*haih m haih…*
easy	容易	*yùhng yi*
difficult	難	*nàahn*
far	遠	*yúhn*
steep	斜	*che*
I'm exhausted.	我好癐喇。	*ngóh hóu guih la*
How far is it to…?	離…有幾遠?	*lèih…yáuh géi yúhn*
Show me on the map, please.	唔該喺地圖上面指畀我睇。	*m gōi hái deih tòuh seuhng mihn jí béi ngóh tái*
I'm lost.	我蕩失路。	*ngóh dohng sāt louh*
Where's…?	…喺邊度?	*…hái bīn douh*
the bridge	橋	*kìuh*
the cave	洞	*duhng*
the cliff	懸崖	*yùhn ngàaih*
the desert	沙漠	*sā mohk*
the farm	農場	*nùhng chèuhng*
the field	農田	*nùhng tìhn*
the forest	森林	*sām làhm*
the mountain	山	*sāan*
the lake	湖	*wùh*

the nature preserve	自然保護區	*jih yìhn bóu wuh kēui*
Where's...?	···喺邊度?	*...hái bīn douh*
the park	公園	*gūng yún*
the path	道路	*douh louh*
the peak	山頂	*sāan déng*
the picnic area	野餐區	*yéh chāan kēui*
the pond	池塘	*chìh tóng*
the river	河流	*hòh làuh*
the sea	大海	*daaih hói*
the stream	小河	*síu hòh*
the thermal spring	溫泉	*wān chyùhn*
the valley	山谷	*sāan gūk*
the viewpoint	觀景點	*gūn gíng dím*
the vineyard	葡萄園	*pòuh tòuh yùhn*
the waterfall	瀑布	*bohk bou*

Going Out

ESSENTIAL

What's there to do at night?	夜晚可以做乜野呢?	*yeh máahn hó yíh jouh māt yéh nē*
Do you have a program of events?	你有冇節目表?	*néih yáuh móuh jit muhk bíu*
What's playing tonight?	今晚做乜野?	*gām máahn jouh māt yéh*
Where's...?	···喺邊度?	*...hái bīn douh*
the downtown area	市中心	*síh jūng sām*
the bar	酒吧	*jáu bā*
the dance club	跳舞俱樂部	*tiu móuh kēui lohk bouh*
Is there a cover charge?	有冇附加費?	*yáuh móuh fuh gā fai*

Entertainment

Can you recommend…?	你可唔可以介紹…? *néih hó m hó yíh gaai siuh…*
a concert	一個音樂會 *yāt go yām ngohk wúi*
a movie	一部電影 *yāt bouh dihn yíng*
an opera	一部歌劇 *yāt bouh gō kehk*
a play	一部戲劇 *yāt bouh hei kehk*
When does it start/end?	幾點開始/結束? *géi dím hōi chí/git chūk*
Where's…?	…喺邊度? *…hái bīn douh*
the concert hall	音樂廳 *yām ngohk tēng*
the opera house	歌劇院 *gō kehk yún*
the theater	劇院 *kehk yún*
I like…	我鍾意… *ngóh jūng yi…*
classical music	古典音樂 *gú dín yām ngohk*
folk music	民族音樂 *màhn juhk yām ngohk*
jazz	爵士樂 *jeuk sih ngohk*
pop music	流行音樂 *làuh hàhng yām ngohk*
rap	說唱 *syut cheung*

Nightlife

What's there to do at night?	夜晚可以做乜野? *yeh máahn hó yíh jouh māt yéh*
Can you recommend…?	你可唔可以介紹…? *néih hó m hó yíh gaai siuh…*
a bar	一個酒吧 *yāt go jáu bā*
a casino	一個賭場 *yāt go dóu chèuhng*
a dance club	跳舞俱樂部 *tiu móuh kēui lohk bouh*
a gay club	一個同性戀俱樂部 *yāt go tùhng sing lyún kēui lohk bouh*
a jazz club	爵士樂俱樂部 *jeuk sih ngohk kēui lohk bouh*

YOU MAY HEAR...

唔該熄手機。 *m gōi sīk sáu gēi*

Turn off your cell [mobile] phones, please.

a club with Chinese music	一間有中國音樂嘅俱樂部 *yāt gāan yáuh jūng gwok yām ngohk ge kēui lohk bouh*
Is there live music?	有冇現場音樂？ *yáuh móuh yihn chèuhng yām ngohk*
How do I get there?	我點樣去嗰度？ *ngóh dím heui gó douh*
Is there a cover charge?	有冇附加費？ *yáuh móuh fuh gā fai*
Let's go dancing.	我哋去跳舞啦。 *ngóè deih heui tiu móuh lā*
Is this area safe at night?	呢個地區夜晚安唔安全？ *nī go deih kēui yeh máahn ōn m ōn chyùhn*

For Tickets, see page 21.

Nightlife is more common in south China than elsewhere; restaurants, bars and cafes usually stay open until at least midnight in the south. However, Hong Kong, which is known as the pearl of the Orient, is a city with a thriving night scene. Bars and dance clubs can be found in major tourist areas and near hotels. English-language newspapers often list cultural ongoings in major cities. Ask about local events at your hotel or check for events listings in a local newspaper.

Special Requirements

Business Travel

ESSENTIAL

I'm here on business.	我喺呢度工幹。	*ngóh hái nī douh gūng gon*
Here's my business card.	呢張係我嘅咭片。	*nī jēung haih ngóh ge kāat pín*
Can I have your card?	可唔可以畀你嘅咭片我？	*hó m̀ hó yíh béi néih ge kāat pín ngóh*
I have a meeting with…	我同⋯有一個會。	*ngóh tùhng…yáuh yāt go wúi*
Where's…?	⋯喺邊度？	*…hái bīn douh*
the business center	商業中心	*sēung yihp jūng sām*
the convention hall	會議廳	*wuih yíh tēng*
the meeting room	會議室	*wuih yíh sāt*

Conducting business in China should be done respectfully. When presenting or receiving a business card in China, hold the card in both hands. If you have just received a card, do not put it away before reading it.

Note that Chinese surnames precede given names, i.e. Li Yang should be referred to as Mr Li. However, some Chinese professionals have adopted Western first names and name order.

On Business

I'm here for a seminar/conference.	我喺呢度開研討會／開會	*ngóh hái nī douh hōi yìhn tóu wúi/hōi wúi*
I'm here for a meeting.	我來呢度開會。	*ngóh làih nī douh hōi wúi*
My name is...	我叫···	*ngóh giu...*
May I introduce my colleague...	我介紹一下同事···	*ngóh gaai siuh yāt háh tùhng sih...*
I have a meeting/ an appointment with...	我同···有一個會／約。	*ngóh tùhng...yáuh yāt go wúi/yeuk*
I'm sorry I'm late.	對唔住我遲到。	*deui m jyuh ngóh chìh dou*
I need an interpreter.	我需要翻譯。	*ngóh sēui yiu fāan yihk*
You can reach me at the...Hotel.	你可以喺···酒店搵到我。	*néih hó yíh hái... jáu dim wán dóu ngóh*
I'm here until...	我要喺呢度留到···	*ngóh yiu hái nī douh làuh dou...*
I need to...	我需要···	*ngóh sēui yiu...*
make a call	打電話	*dá dihn wá*
make a photocopy	影印	*yíng yan*
send an e-mail	發電郵	*faat dihn yàuh*
send a fax	發傳真	*faat chyùhn jān*

| send a package (overnight) | 寄一個（第二日送到嘅）包裹 *gei yāt go (daih yih yaht sung dou ge) bāau gwó* |
| It was a pleasure to meet you. | 好高興見到你。 *hóu gōu hing gin dóu néih* |

For Communications, see page 49.

YOU MAY HEAR...

你有冇預約？ *néih yáuh móuh yuh yeuk*	Do you have an appointment?
同邊個？ *tùhng bīn go*	With whom?
佢開緊會。 *kéuih hōi gán wúi*	He/She is in a meeting.
唔該等一等。 *m gōi dáng yāt dáng*	One moment, please.
唔該坐吓。 *m gōi chóh háh*	Have a seat.
你要唔要飲啲乜野？ *néih yiu m yiu yám dī māt yéh*	Would you like something to drink?
多謝光臨。 *dō jeh gwōng làhm*	Thank you for coming.

ESSENTIAL

Is there a discount for kids?	細蚊仔有冇折？	*sai mān jái yáuh móuh jit*
Can you recommend a babysitter?	你可唔可以介紹一位保姆？	*néih hó m hó yíh gaai siuh yāt wái bóu móuh*
Do you have a child's seat/highchair?	你有冇BB櫈/高櫈？	*néih yáuh móuh bìh bī dang/gōu dang*
Where can I change the baby?	我喺邊度可以幫細蚊仔換尿片？	*ngó hái bīn douh hó yíh bōng sai mān jái wuhn niuh pín*

Out & About

Can you recommend something for kids?	你可唔可以推薦細蚊仔玩嘅活動？	*néih hó m hó yíh tēui jin sai mān jái wáan ge wuht duhng*
Where's...?	…喺邊度？	*...hái bīn douh*
the amusement park	遊樂園	*yàuh lohk yùhn*
the arcade	遊樂場	*yàuh lohk chèuhng*
the kiddie [paddling] pool	兒童泳池	*yìh tùhng wihng chìh*
the park	公園	*gūng yún*
the playground	操場	*chōu chèuhng*
the zoo	動物園	*duhng maht yùhn*
Are kids allowed?	細蚊仔可唔可以入去？	*sai mān jái hó m hó yíh yahp heui*

Is it safe for kids?	細蚊仔玩安唔安全？	*sai mān jái wáan ngōn m ngōn chyùhn*
Is it suitable for... year olds?	適唔適合···歲嘅細蚊仔？	*sīk m sīk hahp... seui ge sai mān jái*

YOU MAY HEAR...

真係可愛！ *jān haih hó ngoi*   How cute!
佢叫乜野名？ *kéuih giu māt yéh méng*   What's his/her name?
佢幾大？ *kéuih géi daaih*   How old is he/she?

Baby Essentials

Do you have...?	你有冇···？	*néih yáuh móuh...*
a baby bottle	奶樽	*náaih jēun*
baby food	嬰兒食品	*yīng yìh sihk bán*
baby wipes	嬰兒紙巾	*yīng yìh jí gān*
a car seat	汽車安全座椅	*hei chē ngōn chyùhn yí*
a children's menu	兒童菜單	*yìh tùhng choi dāan*
a child's seat/ highchair	BB凳/高凳	*bìh bī dang/gōu dang*
a crib/cot	搖籃/床仔	*yìuh láam/chòhng jái*
diapers [nappies]	尿片	*niuh pín*
formula [baby food]	奶粉	*náaih fán*
a pacifier [dummy]	奶嘴	*náaih jéui*
a playpen	遊戲圍欄	*yàuh hei wàih làahn*
a stroller [pushchair]	BB 車	*bìh bī chē*

Can I breastfeed the baby here?	我可唔可以喺呢度餵細蚊仔人奶？	*ngóh hó m hó yíh hái nī douh wai sai mān jái yàhn náaih*
Where can I breastfeed/ change the baby?	我喺邊度可以餵細蚊仔食人奶/幫細蚊仔換尿片？	*ngóh hái bīn douh hó yíh wai sai mān jái sihk yàhn náaih/bōng sai mān jái wuhn niuh pín*

Babysitting

Can you recommend a babysitter?	你可唔可以介紹一位保姆？	*néih hó m hó yíh gaai siuh yāt wái bóu móuh*
What's the charge?	你哋收費係幾多？	*néih deih sāu fai haih géi dō*
I'll be back by…	我喺…之前返嚟。	*ngóh hái…jī chìhn fāan làih*
I can be reached at…	打…可以搵到我。	*dá…hó yíh wán dóu ngóh*

Health & Emergency

Can you recommend a pediatrician?	你可唔可以介紹一位兒科醫生？	*néih hó m hó yíh gaai siuh yāt wái yìh fō yī sāng*
My child is allergic to…	我嘅細蚊仔對…過敏。	*ngóh ge sai mān jái deui…gwo máhn*

My child is missing.	我嘅細蚊仔唔見咗。	*ngóh ge sai mān jái m gin jó*
Have you seen a boy/girl ?	你有冇睇到一個男仔／女仔？	*néih yáuh móuh tái dóu yāt go nàahm jái/néuih já*

For Health, see page 148.

For Police, see page 146.

Disabled Travelers

ESSENTIAL

Is there…?	有冇…？	*yáuh móuh…*
access for the disabled	殘疾人通道	*chàahn jaht yàhn tūng douh*
a wheelchair ramp	輪椅通道	*lèuhn yí tūng douh*
a handicapped-[disabled-] accessible toilet	一間殘疾人可以用嘅洗手間	*yāt gāan chàahn jaht yàhn hó yíh yuhng ge sái sáu gāan*
I need…	我需要…	*ngóh sēui yiu…*
assistance	幫助	*bōng joh*
an elevator [a lift]	電梯	*dihn tāi*
a ground-floor room	一間一樓嘅房	*yāt gāan yāt láu ge fóng*

老幼残孕休息室

For the old , weak & pregnant

Asking for Assistance

I'm…	我… *ngóh…*
disabled	係殘疾人 *haih chàahn jaht yàhn*
visually impaired	視力唔好 *sih lihk m hóu*
hearing impaired/ deaf	聽力唔好/耳聾 *ting lihk m hóu/yíh lùhng*
unable to walk far/ use the stairs	唔可以行好遠/行樓梯 *m hó yíh hàahng hóu yúhn/hàahng làuh tāi*
Please speak louder.	唔該大聲講。 *m gōi daaih sēng góng*
Can I bring my wheelchair?	我可唔可以帶輪椅？ *ngóh m hó yíh daai lèuhn yí*
Are guide dogs permitted?	導盲犬可唔可以入？ *douh màahng hyún hó m hó yíh yahp*
Can you help me?	你可唔可以幫我？ *néih hó m hó yíh bōng ngóh*
Please open/hold the door.	唔該打開/拉著門。 *m gōi dá hōi/lāai jyuh mùhn*

In an
Emergency

ESSENTIAL

Help!	救命！	*gau mehng*
Go away!	走開！	*jáu hōi*
Stop, thief!	唔好走，有賊！	*m hóu jáu yáuh cháak*
Get a doctor!	搵醫生！	*wán yī sāng*
Fire!	著火啦！	*jeuhk fó la*
I'm lost.	我盪失路。	*ngóh dohng sāt louh*
Can you help me?	你可唔可以幫我？	*néih hó m hó yíh bōng ngóh*

In an emergency dial **999** in **Hong Kong**.
In **China** dial:
110 for the police
120 for an ambulance
119 for the fire brigade.

A list of local emergency services numbers should be available at your
hotel or from the tourist information office.

Police

ESSENTIAL

Call the police!	打電話畀警察！	*dá dihn wá béi gíng chaat*
Where's the police station?	警察局喺邊度？	*gíng chaat gúk hái bīn douh*
There was an accident/attack.	有意外／人受襲擊。	*yáuh yi ngoih/yàhn sauh jaahp gīk*
My child is missing.	我嘅細蚊仔唔見咗。	*ngóh ge sai mān jái m gin jó*
I need...	我需要···	*ngóh sēui yiu...*
an interpreter	一個翻譯	*yāt go fāan yihk*
to contact my lawyer	聯絡我嘅律師	*lyùhn lohk ngóh ge leuht sī*
to make a phone call	打電話	*dá dihn wá*
I'm innocent.	我係無辜嘅。	*ngóh haih mouh gū ge*

YOU MAY HEAR...

填好呢份表格。 *tìhn hóu nī fahn bíu gaak*	Fill out this form.
唔該出示你嘅身份證。 *m gōi néih chēut sih néih ge sān fán jing*	Your identification, please.
佢點樣？ *kéuih dím yéung*	What does he/she look like?
係幾時／喺邊度發生？ *haih géi sìh/hái bīn douh faat sāng*	When/Where did it happen?

Crime & Lost Property

I want to report…	我想報告一個…事件。 *ngóh séung bou gou yāt go…sih gín*
a mugging	搶劫 *chéung gip*
a rape	強姦 *kèuhng gāan*
a theft	偷竊 *tāu sit*
I was mugged/ robbed.	我畀人搶野／打劫。 *ngóh béi yàhn chéung yéh/ dá gip*
I lost my…	我嘅…唔見咗。 *ngóh ge…m gin jó*
My…was stolen.	我嘅…畀人偷咗。 *ngóh ge…béi yàhn tāu jó*
backpack	背囊 *bui nòhng*
bicycle	單車 *dāan chē*
camera	相機 *séung gēi*
(hire) car	（租嘅）車 *(jōu ge) chē*
computer	電腦 *dihn nóuh*
credit card	信用卡 *seun yuhng kāat*
jewelry	首飾 *sáu sīk*
money	錢 *chín*
passport	護照 *wuh jiu*
purse [handbag]	銀包 *ngàhn bāau*
traveler's checks [cheques]	旅行支票 *léuih hàhng jī piu*
wallet	銀包 *ngàhn bāau*
I need a police report.	我要報警。 *ngóh yiu bou gíng*
Where is the British/ American/Irish embassy?	英國／美國／愛爾蘭大使館 係邊度？ *yīng gwok /méih gwok/ oi yíh làahn/daaih sí gún haih bīn douh*

For Emergencies, see page 145.

Health

ESSENTIAL

I'm sick [ill].	我病咗。	*ngóh behng jó*
I need an English-speaking doctor.	我需要講英文嘅醫生。	*ngóh sēui yiu góng yīng màhn ge yī sāng*
It hurts here.	呢度痛。	*nī douh tung*
I have a stomachache.	我肚痛。	*ngóh tóu tung*

Finding a Doctor

Can you recommend a doctor/dentist?	你可唔可以介紹一位醫生/牙醫?	*néih hó m hó yíh gaai siuh yāt wái yīsāng/ngàh yī*
Can the doctor come here?	醫生可唔可以嚟呢度?	*yī sāng hó m hó yíh làih nī douh*
I need an English-speaking doctor.	我需要講英文嘅醫生。	*ngóh sēui yiu góng yīng màhn ge yī sāng*
What are the office hours?	辦公時間係幾時?	*baahn gūng sìh gaan haih géi sìh*
I'd like an appointment for...	我想要同···預約。	*ngóh séung yiu tùhng... yuh yeuk*
today	今日	*gām yaht*
tomorrow	聽日	*tīng yaht*
as soon as possible	儘快	*jeuhn faai*
It's urgent.	好急。	*hóu gāpvtv*

For Pharmacy, see page 153.

For Numbers, see page 160.

Symptoms

I'm…	我… *ngóh…*
bleeding	流緊血 *làuh gán hyut*
constipated	便秘 *bihn bei*
dizzy	頭暈 *tàuh wàhn*
nauseous	想嘔 *séung ngáu*
vomiting	嘔 *ngáu*
It hurts here.	呢度痛。 *nī douh tung*
I have…	我… *ngóh…*
an allergic reaction	有過敏反應 *yáuh gwo máhn fáan ying*
chest pain	心口痛 *sām háu tung*
cramps	有抽筋 *yáuh chāu gān*
a cut	有傷口 *yáuh sēung háu*
diarrhea	肚屙 *tóuh ngō*
discharge	排瀉物 *pàaih sit maht*
an earache	耳仔痛 *yíh jái tung*
a fever	發燒 *faat sīu*
pain	痛 *tung*
a rash	出疹 *chēut chán*
a sprain	扭傷 *náu sēung*
some swelling	有腫 *yáuh júng*
a sore throat	喉嚨痛 *hàuh lùhng tung*
a stomachache	肚痛 *tóuh tung*
sunstroke	中暑 *jung syú*
I've been sick [ill] for…days.	我病咗已經…日喇。 *ngóh behng jó yíh gīng… yaht la*

Conditions

I'm anemic.	我有貧血。 *ngóh yáuh pàhn hyut*
I'm allergic to antibiotics.	我對抗生素過敏。 *ngóh deui kong sāng sou gwo máhn*

I have...	我有⋯ *ngóh yáuh...*
arthritis	關節炎 *gwāan jit yìhm*
asthma	哮喘 *hāau chyún*
a heart condition	心臟病 *sām johng behng*
diabetes	糖尿病 *tòhng niuh behng*
high/low blood pressure	高/低血壓 *gōu/dāi hyut ngaat*
I'm epileptic.	我係癲癇患者。 *ngóh haih dīn hàahn waahn jé*
I'm on...	我喺食⋯ *ngóh haih sihk...*

Treatment

Do I need medicine?	我需唔需要食藥? *ngóh sēui m sēui yiu sihk yeuhk*
Can you prescribe a generic drug [unbranded medication]?	你可唔可以開常用藥? *néih hó m hó yíh hōi sèuhng yuhng yeuhk*
Where can I get it?	我喺邊度可以買到? *ngóh hái bīn douh hó yíh máaih dóu*

For What to Take, see page 154.

YOU MAY HEAR...

點樣? *dím yéung*	What's wrong?
邊度痛? *bīn douh tung*	Where does it hurt?
呢度痛唔痛? *nī douh tung m tung*	Does it hurt here?
你食緊藥? *néih sihk gán yeuhk*	Are you on medication?
你對乜野過敏? *néih deui māt yéh gwo máhn*	Are you allergic to anything?
打開口。 *dá hōi háu*	Open your mouth.
深呼吸。 *sām fū kāp*	Breathe deeply.
唔該咳一下。 *m gōi kāt yāt háh*	Cough, please.
去睇專科。 *heui tái jyūn fō*	See a specialist.
去醫院。 *heui yī yún*	Go to the hospital.
你… *néih…*	It's…
骨折 *gwāt jit*	broken
會傳染 *wúih chyùhn yíhm*	contagious
有感染 *yáuh gám yíhm*	infected
扭傷 *náuh sēung*	sprained
唔緊要 *m gán yiu*	nothing serious

Hospital

Notify my family, please.	唔該通知我家人。 *m gōi tūng jī ngóh gā yàhn*
I'm in pain.	我好痛。 *ngóh hóu tung*
I need a doctor/nurse.	我需要醫生/護士。 *ngóh sēui yiu yī sāng / wuh sih*
When are visiting hours?	探病時間係幾時? *taam behng sìh gaan haih géi sìh*
I'm visiting…	我嚟探… *ngóh làih taam…*

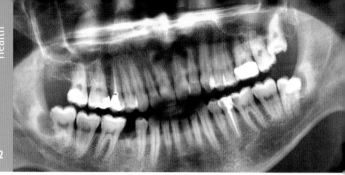

Dentist

I have…	我… *ngóh…*
a broken tooth	有一隻爛牙 *yáuh yāt jek laahn ngàh*
lost a filling	嘅補牙甩咗 *ge bóu ngàh lāt jó*
a toothache	牙痛 *ngàh tung*
Can you fix this denture?	你可唔可以修補呢隻假牙? *néih hó m̀ hó yíh sāu bóu nī jek gá ngàh*

Gynecologist

I have cramps/ a vaginal infection.	我有經期腹痛/陰道感染。 *ngóh yáuh gīng kèih fūk tung/yām douh gám yíhm*
I missed my period.	我月經未嚟。 *ngóh yuht gīng meih làih*
I'm on the Pill.	我食緊避孕藥。 *ngóh sihk gán beih yahn yeuhk*
I'm (…months) pregnant.	我有咗（…月）　　。 *ngóh yáuh jó (…yuht)*
I'm not pregnant.	我冇懷孕。 *ngóh móuh wàaih yahn*
My last period was…	我上次月經係… *ngóh seuhng chi yuht gīng haih…*

Optician

I lost…	我唔見咗··· *ngóh m gin jó…*
a contact lens	隱形眼鏡 *yán yìhng ngáahn géng*
my glasses	我嘅眼鏡 *ngóh ge geng pín*
a lens	一塊鏡片 *yāt faai geng pín*

Payment & Insurance

How much?	幾多錢? *géi dō chín*
Can I pay by credit card?	我可唔可以用信用卡畀錢? *ngóh hó m hó yíh yuhng seun yuhng kāat béi chín*
I have insurance.	我有保險。 *ngóh yáuh bóu hím*
I need a receipt for my insurance.	我需要保險收據。 *ngóh sēui yiu bóu hím sāu geui*

Pharmacy

ESSENTIAL

Where's the pharmacy?	藥房喺邊度? *yeuhk fòhng hái bīn douh*
What time does it open/close?	幾時開門/閂門? *géi sìh hōi mùhn/sāan mùhn*
What would you recommend for…?	你對···有乜野推薦呢? *néih deui…yáuh māt yéh tēui jin nē*
How much do I take?	我要食幾多呢? *ngóh yiu sihk géi dō nē*
Can you fill [make up] this prescription?	你可唔可以提供呢種處方藥? *néih hó m hó yíh tàih gūng nī júng chyúh fōng yeuhk*
I'm allergic to…	我對···敏感。 *ngóh deui…máhn gám*

You will likely find some 24-hour pharmacies in larger cities. Standard pharmacy hours are 9:00 a.m. to 9:00 p.m. In the event of an emergency, visit the nearest hospital emergency center. China is well known for its traditional pharmacies, 中藥 *jūng yeuhk*, which provide many natural remedies: dried and preserved plants, seeds, animal parts and minerals. You may also find acupuncture needles and other holistic healing tools at these locations.

What to Take

How much do I take?	我食幾多呢?	*ngóh sihk géi dō nē*
How often?	幾耐食一次?	*géi noih sihk yāt chi*
Is it safe for children?	對細蚊仔安唔安全?	*deui sai mān jái ngōn m ngōn chyùhn*
I'm taking…	我食緊···	*ngóh sihk gán…*
Are there side effects?	有冇副作用?	*yáuh móuh fu jok yuhng*
I need something for…	我需要醫···嘅藥。	*ngóh sēui yiu yī…ge yeuhk*
a cold	感冒	*gám mouh*
a cough	咳	*kāt*
diarrhea	肚屙	*tóu ngō*
a hangover	宿醉	*sūk jeui*
a headache	頭痛	*tàuh tung*
insect bites	蟲咬	*chùhng ngáauh*
motion sickness	暈浪	*wàhn lohng*
a sore throat	喉嚨痛	*hàuh lùhng tung*
sunburn	曬傷	*saai sēung*
a toothache	牙痛	*ngàh tung*
an upset stomach	腸胃不適	*chuhng waih bāt sīk*

YOU MAY SEE...

一日一次/三次 *yāt yaht yāt chi/sāam chi*	once/three times a day
藥丸 *yeuhk yún*	tablet
滴劑 *dihk jāi*	drop
用茶羹食 *yuhng chàh ngāng sihk*	teaspoon
飯後/飯前/食飯時服用 *faahn hauh/faahn chìhn/ sihk faahn sìh fuhk yuhng*	after/before/with meals
空肚服用整個吞下 *jíng go tān hah*	on an empty stomach swallow whole
使人有睡意 *sí yàhn yáuh seuih yi*	may cause drowsiness
只能外用 *jí nàhng noih yuhng*	for external use only

Basic Supplies

I'd like...	我要··· *ngóh yiu...*
aftershave	鬚後水 *sōu hauh séui*
aspirin	阿斯匹靈 *a sih pāt nìhng*
antiseptic cream	消毒藥膏 *sīu duhk yeuhk gōu*
bandages	繃帶 *bāng dáai*
a comb	一把梳 *yat bá sō*
condoms	避孕套 *beih yahn tou*
contact lens solution	隱形眼鏡藥水 *yán yìhng ngáhn geng yeuhk séui*
deodorant	止汗劑 *jí hohn jāi*
a hairbrush	一把梳 *yāt bá sō*
hairspray	噴髮劑 *pan faat jāi*
insect repellent	殺蟲劑 *saat chùhng jāi*
lotion	乳液 *yúh yihk*

a nail file	指甲銼 *jí gaap cho*
a (disposable) razor	(即棄)剃鬚刀 *(jīk hei) tai sōu dōu*
razor blades	刀片 *dōu pín*
rubbing alcohol [surgical spirit]	外用酒精 *ngoih yuhng jáu jīng*
sanitary napkins [towels]	衛生巾 *waih sāng gān*
shampoo/ conditioner	洗頭水/護髮素 *sái tàuh séui/wuhn faat sou*
soap	番鹼 *fāan gáan*
sunscreen	防曬霜 *fòhng saai sēung*
tampons	棉條 *mìhn tíu*
tissues	紙巾 *jí gān*
toilet paper	廁紙 *chi jí*
a toothbrush	牙刷 *ngàh chaat*
toothpaste	牙膏 *ngàh gōu*

For Baby Essentials, see page 140.

Grammar

Verbs

Chinese verbs are not conjugated. There is one basic verb form that is used for every person and tense. Expressing tense is usually done through adverbs of time such as yesterday and tomorrow:

I walk to school every day. (habitual action)
我每日行路去學校。 *ngóh múih yaht hàahng louh heui hohk haauh*

We want to go to school on foot. (talking about a plan)
我想行路去學校。 *ngóh séung hàahng louh heui hohk haauh*

I walked to school. (talking about a past event)
我係行去學校嘅。 *ngóh haih hàahng heui hohk haauh ge*

Tense can also be expressed by using the particle 過 (*gwo*) or 咗 (*jó*), e.g.,
I have eaten. 我食咗飯喇。 *ngóh sihk jó faahn la*

Nouns

There are no plural forms for Chinese nouns, with few exceptions. Whether the noun is singular or plural is determined from the context or by a number modifying the noun.

My bag is missing.	我嘅袋唔見咗。	*ngóh ge dói m gin jó*
My bags are missing.	我啲袋唔見咗。	*ngóh dī dói m gin jó*

Pronouns

Personal pronouns in Chinese are:

I	我	*ngóh*
you	你	*néih*
he	佢	*kéuih*
she	佢	*kéuih*

it	佢 *kéuih*
we	我哋 *ngóh deih*
you (pl.)	你哋 *néih deih*
they	佢哋 *kéuih deih*

Personal pronouns do not require different verb forms:

I am	我係 *ngóh haih*
He is	佢係 *kéuih haih*
They are	佢哋係 *kéuih deih haih*

Add 嘅 (*ge*) after the pronoun to make it possessive.

| my | 我嘅 *ngóh ge* (Literally: I + ge) |

Word Order

Word order in Chinese is usually as in English: subject, verb, object. This varies, though, depending on the emphasis of the sentence.
I would like a cup of tea.

我想要杯茶。   *ngóh séung yiu būi chàh*

Yes/No questions are formed by using a verb-not-verb structure:

Is this the ticket office? (Literally: Here to be not to be ticket office?)
呢度係唔係售票處?   *nī douh haih m haih sau piu chyu*

Other questions are formed by inserting specific question words (who, what, where, when, how many) in the sentence where the information asked for would come:
Where is the ticket office?
售票處喺邊度?   *sauh piu chyu hái bīn douh*

The Chinese is literally, 'Ticket office is **where**?' '**Where**' follows the verb because the answer would also follow the verb, 'The ticket office is **here**.'

Negation & Affirmation

唔 (*m*) or 冇 (*móuh*) is added before the verb to indicate negation. While 唔 usually preceeds the verb to be, 冇 is used in front of 有 (*yáuh*) and to negate action already completed.

Examples:

I am not on vacation.
我唔係度緊假。
ngóh m haih douh gán ga

I have not bought the ticket.
我仲未買飛。
ngóh juhng meih máaih fēi

Repeat the verb that was used in the question for affirmations or add 唔 (*m*) before the verb for negations.

Would you like tea?
你想唔想飲茶?
néih séung m séung yám chàh

Yes, I would.
想。
séung

No, thank you.
唔想。
m séung

Imperatives

Usually, 啦 (*lā*) or 呀 (*a*) is added at the end of a statement to express a command politely, for example:

Buy the ticket!　　買飛票啦!　　　　　*máaih fēi lā*

Adjectives

Adjectives with two or more syllables in Chinese usually have the character 嘅 (*ge*) at the end and precede the noun they modify, for example:

a good meal　　　好食嘅野　　　*hóu sihk ge yéh*

Adverbs

Adverbs in Chinese are usually followed by 咁 (*gám*) and precede the verbs they modify, for example:

work carefully　　　認真咁工作　　　*yihng jān gám gūng jok*

Numbers

ESSENTIAL

0	零	*lìhng*
1	一	*yāt*
2	二	*yih*
3	三	*sāam*
4	四	*sei*
5	五	*ngh*
6	六	*luhk*
7	七	*chāt*
8	八	*baat*
9	九	*gáu*
10	十	*sahp*
11	十一	*sahp yāt*
12	十二	*sahp yih*
13	十三	*sahp sāam*
14	十四	*sahp sei*
15	十五	*sahp ngh*

16	十六	*sahp luhk*
17	十七	*sahp chāt*
18	十八	*sahp baat*
19	十九	*sahp gáu*
20	二十	*yih sahp*
21	二十一	*yih sahp yāt*
22	二十二	*yih sahp yiih*
30	三十	*sāam sahp*
31	三十一	*sāam sahp yāt*
40	四十	*sei sahp*
50	五十	*ngh sahp*
60	六十	*luhk sahp*
70	七十	*chāt sahp*
80	八十	*baat sahp*
90	九十	*gáu sahp*
100	一百	*yāt baak*
101	一百零一	*yāt baak lìhng yāt*
200	二百	*yih baak*
500	五百	*ngh baak*
1,000	一千	*yāt chīn*
10,000	一萬	*yāt maahn*
1,000,000	一百萬	*yāt baak maahn*

In Chinese, there are general numbers, listed on page 160, used for talking about sums of money, phone numbers, etc. There is also a system for combining a number with an object-specific counter. This system groups objects into types according to shape and size. There are specific ways to count flat objects, machines, animals, people, etc. When you're unsure of the correct counter, you can try using the general numbers above or the all-purpose counters.

All-purpose Counters

1	一個 *yāt go*
2	兩個 *léuhng go*
3	三個 *sāam go*
4	四個 *sei go*
5	五個 *ngh go*
6	六個 *sahp go*
7	七個 *chāt go*
8	八個 *baat go*
9	九個 *gáu go*
10	十個 *sahp go*

Note that the counter usually precedes the word it qualifies, for example:

I'd like an apple.
我想要一個蘋果。
ngóh séung yiu yāt go pìhng gwó

I'd like two apples.
我想要兩個蘋果。
ngóh séung yiu léuhng go pìhng gwó

Other Counters

	thin, flat objects	small objects (of any shape)	packages (of any size)
1	一張 *yāt jēung*	一塊 *yāt faai*	一包 *yāt bāau*
2	兩張 *léuhng jēung*	兩塊 *léuhng faai*	兩包 *léuhng bāau*
3	三張 *sāam jēung*	三塊 *sāam faai*	三包 *sāam bāau*
4	四張 *sei jēung*	四塊 *sei faai*	四包 *sei bāau*
5	五張 *ngh jēung*	五塊 *ngh faai*	五包 *ngh bāau*

Ordinal Numbers

first	第一 *daih yāt*
second	第二 *daih yih*
third	第三 *daih sāam*
fourth	第四 *daih sei*
fifth	第五 *daih ngh*

Measurements of Action

once	一次 *yāt chi*
twice	兩次 *léuhng chi*

Time

ESSENTIAL

What time is it?	幾點? *géi dím*
It's noon [midday].	而家係中午。 *yìh gā haih jūng ngh*
At midnight.	喺午夜。 *hái ngh yeh*
From one o'clock to two o'clock.	由一點到兩點。 *yàuh yāt dím dou léuhng dím*
Five after [past] three.	三點零五分。 *sāam dím lìhng ngh fān*
5:30 a.m./p.m.	上晝/下晝五點半 *seuhng jau/hah jau ngh dím bun*

Days

ESSENTIAL

Monday	星期一 *sīng kèih yāt*
Tuesday	星期二 *sīng kèih yih*
Wednesday	星期三 *sīng kèih sāam*
Thursday	星期四 *sīng kèih sei*
Friday	星期五 *sīng kèih ngh*
Saturday	星期六 *sīng kèih luhk*
Sunday	星期日 *sīng kèih yaht*

Dates

yesterday	琴日 *kàhm yaht*
today	今日 *gām yaht*
tomorrow	聽日 *tīng yaht*
day	日 *yaht*
week	星期 *sīng kèih*
month	月 *yuht*
year	年 *nìhn*

In China, dates are written in the following order: year 年 (*nìhn*),
month 月 (*yuht*) and date 日 (*yaht*). For example, October 12,
2008 in Chinese would be *2008*年*10*月*12*日. Note that while months
can be represented as following, Arabic numbers are also used.

Months

January	一月 *yāt yuht*
February	二月 *yih yuht*
March	三月 *sāam yuht*
April	四月 *sei yuht*

May	五月 *ngh yuht*
June	六月 *luhk yuht*
July	七月 *chāt yuht*
August	八月 *baat yuht*
September	九月 *gáu yuht*
October	十月 *sahp yuht*
November	十一月 *sahp yāt yuht*
December	十二月 *sahp yih yuht*

Seasons

spring	春天 *chēun tīn*
summer	夏天 *hah tīn*
fall [autumn]	秋天 *chāu tīn*
winter	冬天 *dūng tīn*

Holidays

1st Day of the 1st Lunar Month: Spring Festival (Chinese New Year)
May 1: International Labor Day
May 5 (Lunar Calendar): Dragon Boat Festival
October 1: National Day
October 15 (Lunar Calendar): Mid-Autumn Festival (Moon-cake Day)

Traditional holidays, such as Chinese New Year, or Spring
Festival, follow the lunar calendar, so dates vary annually. Chinese
New Year is an important holiday in China, celebrated with gifts,
decorations, traditional food and fireworks. It ends on the fifteenth
day of the lunar new year with the Lantern Festival, which includes
festivities such as a lantern parade and lion dance.

Conversion Tables

When you know	Multiply by	To find
ounces	28.3	grams
pounds	0.45	kilograms
inches	2.54	centimeters
feet	0.3	meters
miles	1.61	kilometers
square inches	6.45	sq. centimeters
square feet	0.09	sq. meters
square miles	2.59	sq. kilometers
pints (U.S./Brit)	0.47/0.56	liters
gallons (U.S./Brit)	3.8/4.5	liters
Fahrenheit	5/9, after −32	Centigrade
Centigrade	9/5, then +32	Fahrenheit

Kilometers to Miles Conversions

1 km – 0.62 mi	20 km – 12.4 mi
5 km – 3.10 mi	50 km – 31.0 mi
10 km – 6.20 mi	100 km – 61.0 mi

Measurement

1 gram	克 hāk	= 0.035 oz.
1 kilogram (kg)	公斤 gūnggān	= 2.2 lb
1 liter (l)	公升 gūng sīng	= 1.06 U.S/0.88 Brit. quarts
1 centimeter (cm)	釐米 lèih mái	= 0.4 inch
1 meter (m)	米 máih	= 39.37 inches/ 3.28 ft.
1 kilometer (km)	公里 gūng léih	= 0.62 mile

Temperature

-40° C – -40° F	-1° C – 30° F	20° C – 68° F
-30° C – -22° F	0° C – 32° F	25° C – 77° F
-20° C – -4° F	5° C – 41° F	30° C – 86° F
-10° C – 14° F	10° C – 50° F	35° C – 95° F
-5° C – 23° F	15° C – 59° F	

Oven Temperature

100° C – 212° F	175° C – 347° F	204° C – 400° F
121° C – 250° F	177° C – 350° F	220° C – 428° F
149° C – 300° F	180° C – 356° F	250° C – 482° F
150° C – 302° F	200° C – 392° F	260° C – 500° F

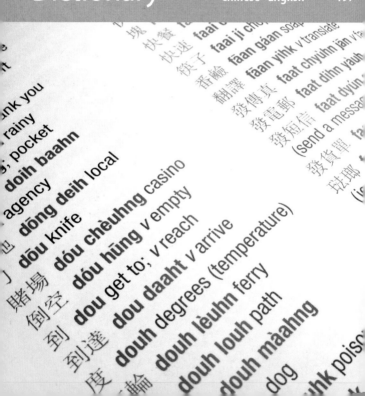

...nk you
...rainy
...; pocket
doih baahn
...agency
dōng deih local
dóu knife
賭場 **dóu chèuhng** casino
倒空 **dóu hūng** v empty
到 **dóu** get to; v reach
到達 **dou daaht** v arrive
度 **douh** degrees (temperature)
...輪 **douh lèuhn** ferry
douh louh path
douh màahng
dog

塊 faai ...
快遞 faai ji ch...
筷子 **faai ji ch...**
香輪 **fāan gáan** soap
翻譯 **fāan yihk** v translate
發傳真 **faat chyùhn jān** v fa...
發電郵 **faat dihn yàuh**
發短信 **faat dyún ...**
(send a messa...
發貨單 fa...
琺瑯 (is...

A

accept *v* 接受 *jip sauh*

access 進入 *jeun yahp*

accident 意外 *yi ngoih*

accommodation 住宿 *jyuh sūk*

account 帳戶 *jeung wuh*

acupuncture 針灸 *jām gau*

adapter 變壓器 *bin ngaat hei*

address 地址 *deih jí*

admission 入場 *yahp chèuhng*

after 以後 *yíh hauh*

aftershave 鬚後水 *sōu hauh séui*

age 年齡 *nìhn nìhng*

agency 代辦處 *doih baahn chyu*

air conditioning 冷氣 *láahng hei*

air pump 氣泵 *hei bām*

airline 航空公司 *hòhng hūng gūng sī*

airmail 航空信 *hòhng hūng seun*

airplane 飛機 *fēi gēi*

airport 飛機場 *fēi gēi chèuhng*

aisle seat 路口位 *louh háu wái*

allergic 敏感 *máhn gám*

allergic reaction 過敏反應 *gwo máhn fáan ying*

allow *v* 准許 *jéun héui*

alone 單獨 *dāan duhk*

alter *v* (clothing) 改 *gói*

alternate route 更改路線 *gāng gói louh sin*

aluminum foil 錫紙 *sehk jí*

amazing 令人驚奇嘅 *lihng yàhn gīng kèih ge*

ambulance 救護車 *gau sēung chē*

American 美國人 *méih gwok yàhn*

amusement park 遊樂園 *yàuh lohk yùhn*

anemic 貧血 *pàhn hyut*

anesthesia 麻醉 *màh jeui*

animal 動物 *duhng maht*

ankle 腳眼 *geuk ngáahn*

antibiotic 抗生素 *kong sāng sou*

antiques store 古董店 *gú dúng dim*

antiseptic cream 消毒藥膏 *sīu duhk yeuk gōu*

anything 任何野 *yahm hòh yéh*

apartment 公寓 *gūng yuh*

appendix (body part) 盲腸

---

adj adjective	**BE** British English	**prep** preposition
adv adverb	**n** noun	**v** verb

màahng chéung

appetizer 開胃菜 *hōi waih choi*

appointment 約 *yeuk*

area code 區號 *kēui houh*

arm 手臂 *sáu bei*

aromatherapy 香薰療法 *hēung fān lìuh faat*

around (the corner) 轉角處 *jyun gok chyu*

arrivals (airport) 抵達 *dái daaht*

arrive v 到達 *dou daaht*

artery 動脈 *duhng mahk*

arthritis 關節炎 *gwāan jit yìhm*

Asian (restaurant) 亞洲 *nga jāu*

aspirin 阿斯匹零 *a sī pāt lìhng*

asthmatic 氣喘 *hei chyún*

ATM 自動提款機 *jih duhng tàih fún gēi*

ATM card 自動提款卡 *jih duhng tàih fún kāat*

attack (on person) 攻擊 *gūng gīk*

attend v 出席 *chēut jihk*

attraction (place) 遊覽勝地 *yàuh láahm sing deih*

attractive 有吸引力嘅 *yáuh kāp yáhn lihk ge*

Australia 澳洲 *ou jāu*

B

baby BB *bìh bī*

baby bottle 奶樽 *náaih jēung*

baby wipe 嬰兒紙巾 *yīng yìh jí gān*

babysitter 保姆 *bóu móuh*

back (body part) 背脊 *bui jek*

backache 背痛 *bui tung*

backpack 背囊 *bui nòhng*

bag 袋 *dói*

baggage [BE] 行李 *hàhng léih*

baggage claim 行李認領 *hàhng léih yihng léhng*

baggage ticket 行李票 *hàhng léih piu*

bakery 麵包鋪 *mihn bāau póu*

ballet 芭蕾 *bā lèuih*

bandage 繃帶 *bāng dáai*

bank 銀行 *ngàhn hòhng*

bar (place) 酒吧 *jáu bā*

barbecue 烤肉 *hāau yuhk*

barber 理髮師 *léih faat sī*

baseball 棒球 *páahng kàuh*

basket (grocery store) 購物籃 *kau maht láam*

basketball 籃球 *làahm kàuh*

bathroom 沖涼房 *chūng lèuhng fóng*

battery 電芯 *dihn sām*

battleground 戰場 *jin chèuhng*

be v 會係 *wúih haih*

beach 海灘 *hói tāan*

beautiful 靚 *leng*

bed 床 *chòhng*

bed and breakfast 有早餐嘅酒店 *yáuh jóu chāan ge jáu dim*

begin v 開始 *hōi chí*

before 以前 *yíh chìhn*

beginner (skill level) 初學者 *chō hohk jé*

behind (direction) 後面 *hauh mihn*

beige 米黃色 *máih wòhng sīk*

belt 皮帶 *pèih dáai*

berth 鋪位 *pou wái*

best 最好 *jeui hóu*

better 好啲 *hóu dī*

bicycle 單車 *dāan chē*

big 大 *daaih*

bike route 單車路線 *dāan chē louh sin*

bikini 比基尼裝 *béi gīn nèih jōng*

bill v (charge) 開單 *hōi dāan;* n (money) 紙幣 *jí baih;* n (of sale) 單 *dāan*

bird 雀仔 *jeuk jái*

birthday 生日 *sāang yaht*

black 黑色 *hāk sīk*

bladder 膀胱 *pòhng gwōng*

bland 無味 *mòuh meih*

blanket 毯 *jīn*

bleed v 流血 *làuh hyut*

blood 血液 *hyut yihk*

blood pressure 血壓 *hyut ngaat*

blouse 女裝恤衫 *néuih jōng sēut*

blue 藍色 *làahm sīk*

board v 登機 *dāng gēi*

boarding pass 登機証 *dāng gēi jing*

boat 船 *syùhn*

bone 骨頭 *gwāt tàuh*

book 書 *syū*

bookstore 書店 *syū dim*

boots 靴 *hēu*

boring 無聊嘅 *mòuh lìuh ge*

botanical garden 植物園 *jihk maht yùhn*

bother v 打擾 *dá gáau*

bottle 樽 *jēun*

bottle opener 開瓶器 *hōi pìhng hei*

bowl 碗 *wún*

box 箱 *sēung*

boxing match 拳擊比賽 *kyùhn gīk béi choi*

boy 男仔 *nàahm jái*

boyfriend 男朋友 *nàahm pàhng yáuh*

bra 胸圍 *hūng wàih*

bracelet 手扼 *sáu ngáak*

break v (tooth) 爛 *laahn*

break-in (burglary) 闖入 *chóng yahp*

breakdown 故障 *gu jeung*

breakfast 早餐 *jóu chāan*

breast 乳房 *yúh fòhng*

breastfeed 餵母乳 *wai móuh yúh*

breathe v 呼吸 *fū kāp*

bridge 橋樑 *kìuh lèuhng*

briefs (clothing) 緊身褲 *gán sān fu*

bring v 帶嚟 *daai làih*

British 英國人 *yīng gwok yàhn*

broken 爛咗 *laahn jó*

brooch 心口針 *sām háu jām*

broom 尋把 *sou bá*

brother 兄弟 *hīng daih*

brown 咖啡色 *ga fē sīk*

bug 蟲 *chùhng*

building 大廈 *daaih hah*

burn v 燒 *sīu*

bus 巴士 *bā sí*

bus station 巴士站 *bā sí jaahm*

bus stop 巴士站 *bā sí jaahm*

bus ticket 巴士車票 *bā sí chē piu*

bus tour 巴士遊覽 *bā sí yàuh láahm*

business 商務 *sēung mouh*

business card 咭片 *kāat pín*

business center 商業中心 *sēung yihp jūng sām*

business class 商務艙 *sēung mouh chōng*

business hours 營業時間 *yìhng yihp sìh gaan*

buttocks 屁股 *pei gú*

buy v 買 *máaih*

bye 再見 *joi gin*

C

cabin 客艙 *haak chōng*

café 咖啡館 *ga fē gún*

call v 打電話 *dá dihn wá*; n 電話 *dihn wá*

calligraphy supplies 書法用品 *syū faat yuhng bán*

calories 卡路里 *kā louh léih*

camera 相機 *séung gēi*

camera case 相機套 *séung gēi tou*

camera store 攝影器材商店 *sip yíng hei chòih sēung dim*

camp v 露營 *louh yìhng*

camping stove 露營爐 *louh yìhng lòuh*

campsite 營地 *yìhng deih*

can opener 開罐器 *hōi gun hei*

Canada 加拿大 *ga nàh daaih*

cancel v 取消 *chéui sīu*

canyon 峽谷 *haap gūk*

car 汽車 *hei chē*

car hire [BE] 出租汽車 *chēut jōu hei chē*

car park [BE] 停車場 *tìhng chē chèuhng*

car rental 出租汽車 *chēut jōu hei chē*

car seat 汽車座位 *hei chē joh wái*

carafe 碴 *jā*

card 卡 *kāat*

carry-on 手提行李 *sáu tàih hàhng léih*

cart (grocery store) 手推車 *sáu tēui chē*

cart (luggage) 行李車 *hàhng léih chē*

case (amount) 件 *gihn*

cash v 換現金 *wuhn yihn gām*; n 現金 *yihn gām*

cash advance 預支現金 *yuh jī yìhn gām*

cashier 出納員 *chēut naahp yùhn*

casino 賭場 *dóu chèuhng*

castle 城堡 *sìhng bóu*

cathedral 大教堂 *daaih gaau tòhng*

cave 山洞 *sāan duhng*

CD CD *sī dī*

cell phone 手機 *sáu gēi*

Celsius 攝氏 *sip sih*

centimeter 釐米 *lèih máih*

ceramic spoon 湯羹 *tōng gāng*

certificate 證明 *jing mìhng*

chair 凳 *dang*

change v (buses) 換車 *wuhn chē*; v (money) 換錢 *wuhn chín*; v (baby) 換尿片 *wuhn niuh pín*; n (money) 散紙 *sáan jí*

charcoal 木炭 *muhk taan*

charge v (credit card) 用信用卡畀錢 *yuhng seun yuhng kāa béi chín*; n (cost) 收費 *sāu fai*

cheap 平 *pèhng*

check v (something) 檢查 *gím chàh*; v (luggage) 托運 *tok wahn*; n (payment) 支票 *jī piu*

check-in (airport) 辦理登機手續 *baahn léih dāng gēi sáu juhk*

checking account 支票戶口 *jī piu wuh háu*

check-out (hotel) 退房 *teui fóng*

chemist [BE] 藥劑師 *yeuhk jāi sī*

cheque [BE] 支票 *jī piu*

chest (body part) 心口 *sām háu*

chest pain 心口痛 *sām háu tung*

chewing gum 香口膠 *hēung háu gāau*

child 細蚊仔 *sai mān jái*

child's seat BB凳 *bìh bī dang*

children's menu 兒童菜單 *yìh tùhng choi dāan*

children's portion 兒童飯量 *yìh tùhng faahn leuhng*

china 瓷器 *chìh hei*

China 中國 *jūng gwok*

Chinese 中文 *jūng màhn*

Chinese painting 中國畫 *jūng gwok wá*

chopsticks 筷子 *faai jí*

church 教堂 *gaau tóng*

cigar 雪茄 *syut kā*

cigarette 煙 *yīn*

class 艙 *chōng*

clay pot 砂鍋 *sā wō*

cloisonné 景泰藍 *gíng taai làahm*

first class 頭等艙 *tàuh dáng chōng*

classical music 古典音樂 *gú dín yām ngohk*

clean v 洗 *sái*; adj 乾淨 *gōn jehng*

cleaning product 清潔產品 *chīng git cháan bán*

clear v (on an ATM) 清除 *chīng chèuih*

cliff 懸崖 *yùhn ngàaih*

cling film [BE] 保鮮紙 *bóu sīn jí*

close v (a shop) 關門 *gwāan mùhn*; adj 近 *kahn*

closed 關閉 *gwāan bai*

clothing 衣物 *yī maht*

clothing store 時裝店 *sìh jōng dim*

club 俱樂部 *kēui lohk bouh*

coat 外套 *ngoih tou*

coffee shop 咖啡店 *ga fē dim*

coin 硬幣 *ngaahng beih*

cold (sickness) 感冒 *gám mouh*; (temperature) 冷 *láahng*

colleague 同事 *tùhng sih*

cologne 古龍水 *gú lùhng séui*

color 顏色 *ngàahn sīk*

comb 梳 *sō*

come v 嚟 *làih*

complaint 投訴 *tàuh sou*

computer 電腦 *dihn nóuh*

concert 音樂會 *yām ngohk wúi*

concert hall 音樂廳 *yām ngohk tēng*

condition (medical) 症狀 *jing johng*

conditioner 護髮素 *wuh faat sou*

condom 避孕套 *beih yan tou*

conference 會議 *wuih yíh*

confirm v 證實 *jing saht*

congestion 充血 *chūng hyut*

connect v (internet) 連接 *lìhn jip*

connection (internet) 連接 *lìhn jip*; (flight) 轉機 *jyun gēi*

constipated 便秘 *bin bei*

consulate 領事館 *líhng sih gún*

consultant 顧問 *gu mahn*

contact v 聯繫 *lyùhn haih*

contact lens 隱形眼鏡 *yán yìhng ngáahn géng*

contact lens solution 隱形眼鏡液 *yán yìhng ngáahn géng yihk*

contagious 傳染嘅 *chyùhn yíhm ge*

convention hall 會議廳 *wuih yíh tēng*

cook v 烹調 *pāang tìuh*

cooking gas 烹調煤氣 *pāang*

tiuh mùih hei

cool (temperature) 涼 *lèuhng*

copper 銅 *tùhng*

corkscrew 開酒器 *hōi jáu hei*

cost v 用 *yuhng*

cot 床仔 *chòhng jái*

cotton 棉花 *mìhn fā*

cough n/v 咳 *kāt*

country code 國家代號 *gwok gā doih houh*

cover charge 附加費 *fuh gā fai*

crash v (car) 撞 *johng*

cream (ointment) 藥膏 *yeuhk gōu*

credit card 信用卡 *seun yuhng kāat*

crib 搖籃 *yìuh láam*

crystal 水晶 *séui jīng*

cup 杯 *būi*

currency 貨幣 *fo baih*

currency exchange 貨幣兌換 *fo baih deui wuhn*

currency exchange office 貨幣兌換局 *fo baih deui wuhn gúk*

current account [BE] 支票戶口 *jī piu wuh háu*

customs 海關 *hói gwāan*

cut v (hair) 剪 *jín*; n (injury) 傷口 *sēung háu*

cute 得意 *dāk yi*

cycling 踩單車 *cháai dāan chē*

D

damage v 損傷 *syún sēung*

damaged 壞咗 *waaih jó*

dance v 跳舞 *tiu móuh*

dance club 舞蹈俱樂部 *móuh douh kēui lohk bouh*

dangerous 危險 *ngàih hím*

dark 黑暗 *hāk ngam*

date (calendar) 日期 *yaht kèih*

day 日 *yaht*

deaf 聾 *lùhng*

debit card 借記卡 *je gei kāat*

declare v 申報 *sān bou*

decline v (credit card) 拒絕 *kéuih jyuht*

degrees (temperature) 度 *douh*

delay v 遲啲 *chìh dī*

delete v 刪除 *sāan chèuih*

delicatessen 熟食 *suhk sihk*

delicious 好食 *hóu sihk*

denim 牛仔布 *ngàuh jái bou*

dentist 牙醫 *ngàh yī*

denture 假牙 *gá ngàh*

deodorant 止汗劑 *jí hon jāi*

department store 百貨公司 *baak fo gūng sī*

departure 離開 *lèih hōi*

deposit v 存錢 *chyùhn chín*; n (bank) 儲蓄 *chyúh chūk*

desert 沙漠 *sā mohk*

diabetic 糖尿病 *tòhng niuh behng*

dial v 撥號 *buht houh*

diamond 鑽石 *jyun sehk*

diaper 尿片 *niuh pín*

diarrhea 肚屙 *tóu ngō*

diesel 柴油 *chàih yàuh*

difficult 困難 *kwan nàahn*

digital 數碼 *sou máh*

digital camera 數碼相機 *sou máh séung gēi*

digital photo 數碼相片 *sou máh seung pín*

digital print 數碼印刷品 *sou máh yan chaat bán*

dining room 飯廳 *faahn tēng*

dinner 晚餐 *máahn chāan*

direction 方向 *fōng heung*

dirty 污糟 *wū jōng*

disabled 殘疾 *chàahn jaht*

disabled accessible [BE] 殘疾人通道 *chàahn jaht yàhn tūng douh*

disconnect (computer) 斷開 *tyúhn hōi*

discount 折 *jit*

dish (kitchen) 碟 *dihp*

dishwasher 洗碗機 *sái wún gēi*

dishwashing liquid 洗潔精 *sái git jīng*

display 顯示 *hín sih*

display case 陳列櫃 *chàhn liht gwaih*

disposable 即棄 *jīk hei*

disposable razor 即棄剃鬚刀 *jīk hei tai sōu dōu*

dive v 潛水 *chìhm séui*

diving equipment 潛水用具 *chìhm séui yuhng geuih*

divorce v 離婚 *lèih fān*

dizzy 頭暈眼花 *tàuh wàhn ngáahn fā*

doctor 醫生 *yī sāng*

doll 公仔 *gūng jái*

dollar (H.K.) 港元 *góng yùhn*; **(U.S.)** 美元 *méih yùhn*

domestic 國內 *gwok noih*

domestic flight 國內航班 *gwok noih hòhng bāan*

dormitory 宿舍 *sūk se*

double bed 雙人床 *sēung yàhn chòhng*

downtown 市中心 *síh jūng sām*

dozen 一打 *yāt dā*

dress (piece of clothing) 禮服 *láih fuhk*

dress code 服裝要求 *fuhk jōng yīu kàuh*

drink v 飲 *yám*; n 飲料 *yám liuh*

drink menu 飲料單 *yám liuh dāan*

drive v 開車 *hōi chē*

driver's license number 駕駛執照號碼 *ga sái jāp jiu houh máh*

drop (medicine) 滴 *dihk*

drowsiness 睡意 *seuih yi*

dry cleaner 乾洗店 *gōn sái dim*
during 期間 *kèih gāan*
duty (tax) 關稅 *gwāan seui*
duty-free 免稅 *mín seui*
DVD DVD *dī wī dī*

E

ear 耳仔 *yíh jái*
earache 耳仔痛 *yíh jái tung*
early 早 *jóu*
earrings 耳環 *yíh wáan*
east 東部 *dūng bouh*
easy 容易 *yùhng yih*
eat *v* 食 *sihk*
economy class 經濟艙 *gīng jai chōng*
elbow 手掙 *sáu jāang*
electric outlet 電制 *dihn jai*
elevator 電梯 *dihn tāi*
e-mail *v* 發電郵 *faat dihn yàuh; n* 電子郵件 *dihn jí yàuh gín*
e-mail address 電郵地址 *dihn yàuh deih jí*
emergency 緊急狀態 *gán gāp johng taai*
emergency exit 緊急出口 *gán gāp chēut háu*
empty *v* 倒空 *dóu hūng*
enamel (jewelry) 琺瑯 *faat lòhng*
end *v* 結束 *git chūk*
English 英文 *yīng màhn*

engrave *v* 雕刻 *dīu hāk*
enjoy *v* 享用 *héung yuhng*
enter *v* 進入 *jeun yahp*
entertainment 娛樂 *yùh lohk*
entrance 入口 *yahp háu*
envelope 信封 *seun fūng*
epileptic 癲癇 *dīn gáan*
equipment 設備 *chit beih*
escalator 自動扶梯 *jih duhng fùh tāi*
e-ticket 電子票 *dihn jí piu*
evening 夜晚 *yeh máahn*
excess 超過 *chīu gwo*
exchange *v (money)* 兌換 *deui wuhn; v (goods)* 交換 *gāau wuhn; n (place)* 換地方 *wuhn deih fong*
exchange rate 兌換率 *deui wuhn léut*
excursion 遊覽 *yàuh láahm*
excuse *v* 原諒 *yùhn leuhng*
exhausted 用盡 *yuhng jeuhn*
exit *v* 出去 *chēut heui; n* 出口 *chēut háu*
expensive 昂貴 *ngòhng gwai*
expert (skill level) 專家 *jyūn gā*
exposure (film) 曝光 *bouh gwōng*
express 快 *faai*
extension (phone) 分機 *fān gēi*
extra 額外 *ngaak ngoih*
extra large 加大碼 *gā daaih máh*

extract v (tooth) 剝 mōk
eye 眼 ngáahn

F

face 面 mihn
facial 面部 mihn bouh
family 家庭 gā tìhng
fan (appliance) 電風扇 dihn fūng sin
far 遠 yúhn
far-sighted 遠視 yúhn sih
farm 農場 nùhng chèuhng
fast 快速 faai chūk
fast food 快餐 faai chāan
fat free 無脂肪 mòuh jī fōng
father 父親 fuh chān
fax v 發傳真 faat chyùhn jān; n 傳真 chyùhn jān
fax number 傳真號碼 chyùhn jān houh máh
fee 費用 fai yuhng
feed v 餵 wai
ferry 渡輪 douh lèuhn
fever 發燒 faat sīu
field (sports) 運動場 wahn duhng chèuhng
fill out v (form) 填寫 tìhn sé
film (camera) 菲林 fēi lám
fine (fee) 罰款 faht fún
finger 手指 sáu jí
fingernail 指甲 jí gaap

fire 火 fó
fire department 消防隊 sīu fòhng yùhn
fire door 防火門 fòhng fó mùhn
first 第一 daih yāt
first class 頭等艙 tàuh dáng chōng
fit (clothing) 適合 sīk hahp
fitting room 試身室 si sān sāt
fix v (repair) 修理 sāu léih
fixed-price menu 價格固定嘅菜單 ga gaak gu dihng ge choi dāan
flashlight 電筒 dihn túng
flight 航班 hòhng bāan
floor 地板 deih báan
florist 賣花人 maaih fā yàhn
flower 花 fā
folk music 民間音樂 màhn gāan yām ngohk
food 食物 sihk maht
foot 腳 geuk
football game [BE] 足球賽 jūk kàuh choi
for 為咗 waih jó
forecast 預報 yuh bou
forest 森林 sām làhm
fork 叉 chā
form (fill-in) 表格 bíu gaak
formula (baby) 奶粉 náaih fán
fort 要塞 yiu choi
fountain 噴水池 pan séui chìh

free 免費 *mín fai*
freezer 雪櫃 *syut gwaih*
fresh 新鮮 *sān sīn*
friend 朋友 *pàhng yáuh*
frying pan 煎鍋 *jīn wō*
full-service 全面服務 *chyùhn mihn fuhk móuh*

G

game 遊戲 *yàuh hei*
garage 車房 *chē fòhng*
garbage 垃圾 *laahp saap*
garbage bag 垃圾袋 *laahp saap dói*
gas 汽油 *hei yàuh*
gas station 加油站 *gā yàuh jaahm*
gate [airport] 登機門 *dāng gēi mùhn*
get off (a train/bus/subway) 落車 *lohk chē*
gift 禮物 *láih maht*
gift shop 禮品店 *láih bán dim*
girl 女仔 *néuih jái*
girlfriend 女朋友 *néuih pàhng yáuh*
give *v* 畀 *béi*
glass (drinking) 玻璃杯 *bō lēi būi*
glasses (optical) 眼鏡 *ngáahn géng*
go *v* **(somewhere)** 去 *heui*
gold 金 *gām*

golf course 高爾夫球場 *gōu yíh fū kàuh chèuhng*
golf tournament 高爾夫球比賽 *gōu yíh fū kàuh béi choi*
good *adj/n* 好 *hóu*
good evening 晚安 *máahn ngōn*
good morning 早晨 *jóu sàhn*
goodbye 再見 *joi gin*
goods 貨物 *fo maht*
gram 克 *hāk*
grandchild 孫 *syūn*
grandparent 祖父母 *jóu fuh móuh*
gray 灰色 *fūi sīk*
green 綠色 *luhk sīk*
grocery store 雜貨店 *jaahp fo dim*
ground floor 一樓 *yāt láu*
group 小組 *síu jóu*
guide 指南 *jí nàahm*
guide book 指南 *jí nàahm*
guide dog 導盲犬 *douh màahng hyún*
gym 體操 *tái chōu*
gynecologist 婦產科醫生 *fúh cháan fō yī sāng*

H

hair 頭髮 *tàuh faat*
hair dryer 風筒 *fūng túng*
hair salon 髮廊 *faat lòhng*
hairbrush 梳 *sō*

haircut 飛髮 *fēi faat*

hairspray 噴髮劑 *pan faat jāi*

hairstyle 髮型 *faat yìhng*

hairstylist 髮型師 *faat yìhng sī*

halal 清真食品 *chīng jān sihk bán*

half 半 *bun*

half hour 半小時 *bun síu sìh*

half-kilo 半公斤 *bun gūng gān*

hammer 錘 *chéui*

hand 手 *sáu*

hand luggage 手提行李 *sáu tàih hàhng léih*

handbag [BE] 手袋 *sáu dói*

handicapped 殘疾 *chàahn jaht*

handicapped-accessible 殘疾人通道 *chàahn jaht yàhn tūng douh*

hangover 宿醉 *sūk jeui*

happy 愉快 *yuh faai*

hat 帽 *móu*

have *v* 做 *jouh*

hay fever 花粉症 *fān fán jing*

head (body part) 頭 *tàuh*

headache 頭痛 *tàuh tung*

headphones 耳筒 *yíh túng*

health 健康 *gihn hōng*

health food store 健康食品店 *gihn hōng sihk bán dim*

hearing impaired 聽力唔好 *ting lihk m̀h hóu*

heart 心臟 *sām johng*

heart condition 心臟狀況 *sām johng johng fong*

heat 加熱 *gā yiht*

heater 加熱器 *gā yiht hei*

heating [BE] 暖氣 *nyúhng hei*

hello 你好 *néih hóu*

helmet 頭盔 *tàuh kwāi*

help 幫助 *bōng joh*

here 呢度 *nī douh*

hi 你好 *néih hóu*

high 高 *gōu*

highchair 高腳椅 *gōu geuk yí*

highway 高速公路 *gōu chūk gūng louh*

hill 山仔 *sāan jái*

hire *v* **[BE]** 雇用 *gu yuhng*

hire car [BE] 租用汽車 *jōu yuhng hei chē*

hitchhike *v* 搭車 *daap chē*

hockey 曲棍球 *kūk gwan kàuh*

holiday [BE] 假期 *ga kèih*

horse track 跑馬場 *páau máh chèuhng*

hospital 醫院 *yī yún*

hostel 旅舍 *léuih se*

hot (temperature) 熱 *yiht;* **(spicy)** 辣 *laaht*

hot spring 溫泉 *wān chyùhn*

hotel 酒店 *jáu dim*

hour 小時 *síu sìh*

house 屋 *ngūk*

housekeeping services 客房清

潔服 務 haak fóng chīng git fuhk mòuh

how 點樣 dím yéung

how much 幾多 géi dō

hug v 攬 láam

hungry 餓 ngoh

hurt 痛 tung

husband 老公 lóuh gūng

I

ice 冰 bīng

ice hockey 冰球 bīng kàuh

icy 冰冷 bīng láahng

identification 證件 jing gín

ill [BE] 病 behng

in 喺 hái

include v 包括 bāau kwut

indoor pool 室內泳池 sāt noih wihng chìh

inexpensive 唔貴 m gwai

infected 傳染 chyùhn yíhm

information (phone) 信息 seun sīk

information desk 訊問處 sēun mahn chyu

insect bite 蟲咬 chùhng ngáau

insect repellent 殺蟲劑 saat chùhng jāi

insert v (on an ATM) 插入 chaap yah

insomnia 失眠 sāt mìhn

instant message 即時訊息 jīk sìh seun sīk

insulin 胰島素 yìh dóu sou

insurance 保險 bóu hím

insurance card 保險卡 bóu hím kāat

insurance company 保險公司 bóu hím gūng sī

interesting 有趣 yáuh cheui

international (airport area) 國際 gwok jai

international flight 國際航班 gwok jai hòhng bāan

international student card 國際學生 證 gwok jai hohk sāang jing

internet 互聯網 wuh lyùhn móhng

internet cafe 網吧 móhng bā

internet service 互聯網服務 wuh lyùhn móhng fuhk mouh

interpreter 口譯員 háu yihk yùhn

intersection 十字路口 sahp jih louh háu

intestine 腸 chéung

introduce v 介紹 gaai siuh

invoice 發貨單 faat fo dāan

Ireland 愛爾蘭 ngoi yíh làahn

Irish 愛爾蘭人 ngoi yíh làahn yàhn

iron v 熨衫 tong sāam; n 熨斗 tong dáu

J

jacket 褸 *lāu*

jade 玉 *yúk*

jar 碴 *jā*

jaw 下爬 *hah pàh*

jazz 爵士樂 *jeuk sih ngohk*

jazz club 爵士樂俱樂部 *jeuk sih ngohk kēui lohk bouh*

jeans 牛仔褲 *ngáuh jái fu*

jeweler 珠寶商 *jyū bóu sēung*

jewelry 首飾 *sáu sīk*

join v 加入 *gā yahp*

joint (body part) 關節 *gwāan jit*

K

key 鑰匙 *só sìh*

key card 鑰匙卡 *só sìh kāat*

key ring 鑰匙扣 *só sìh kau*

kiddie pool 兒童泳池 *yìh tùhng wihng chìh*

kidney (body part) 腎臟 *sahn johng*

kilogram 公斤 *gūng gān*

kilometer 公里 *gūng léih*

kiss v 錫 *sek*

kitchen 廚房 *chyùh fóng*

kitchen foil [BE] 廚房錫紙 *chyùh fóng sehk jí*

knee 膝頭 *sāt tàuh*

knife 刀 *dōu*

kosher 猶太食品 *yàuh taai sihk bán*

L

lace 鞋帶 *hàaih dáai*

lacquerware 漆器 *chāt hei*

lactose intolerant 乳糖過敏 *yúh tòhng gwo máhn*

lake 湖 *wùh*

large 大 *daaih*

last 最後 *jeui hauh*

late (time) 遲咗 *chìh jó*

launderette [BE] 洗衣店 *sái yī dim*

laundromat 洗衣店 *sái yī dim*

laundry 要洗嘅衫 *yiu sái ge sāam*

laundry facility 洗衣店設施 *sái yī dim chit sī*

laundry service 洗衣服務 *sái yī fuhk mouh*

lawyer 律師 *leuht sī*

leather 皮 *péi*

leave v 起飛 *héi fēi*

left (direction) 左邊 *jó bīn*

leg 腿 *téui*

lens 鏡片 *geng pín*

less 比較少 *béi gaau síu*

lesson 課程 *fo chìhng*

letter 信件 *seun gín*

library 圖書館 *tòuh syū gún*

life jacket 救生衣 *gau sāng yī*

lifeguard 救生員 *gau sāng yùhn*

lift v 搭車 *daap chē;* n [BE] 電梯 *dihn tāi*

light (overhead) 燈 *dāng*;
  (cigarette) 點 *dím*
lightbulb 燈膽 *dāng dáam*
lighter 打火機 *dá fó gēi*
like *v* 鍾意 *jūng yi*
line (train) 線 *sin*
linen 麻布 *màh bou*
lip 嘴唇 *jéui sèuhn*
liquor store 酒店 *jáu dim*
liter 公升 *gūng sīng*
little 少少 *síu síu*
live *v* 住 *jyuh*
liver (body part) 肝臟 *gōn johng*
loafers 遊蕩者 *yàuh dong jé*
local 當地 *dōng deih*
lock *n* 鎖 *só*
locker 衣物櫃 *yī maht gwaih*
log on 登錄 *dāng luhk*
log off 退出 *teui chēut*
long 長 *chèuhng*
long sleeves 長袖 *chèuhng jauh*
long-sighted [BE] 有遠見 *yáuh yúhn gin*
look *v* 睇 *tái*
lose *v* **(something)** 唔見咗 *m gin jó*
lost 失去 *sāt heui*
lost and found 失物認領處 *sāt maht yihng líhng chyu*
lotion 化妝乳液 *fa jōng yúh yihk*
love *n/v* **(someone)** 愛 *ngoi*

low 低 *dāi*
luggage 行李 *hàhng léih*
luggage cart 行李推車 *hàhng léih tēui chē*
luggage locker 行李暫存箱 *hàhng léih jaahm chyùhn sēung*
luggage ticket 行李票 *hàhng léih piu*
lunch 午餐 *ngh chāan*
lung 肺 *fai*

M

magazine 雜誌 *jaahp ji*
magnificent 壯觀 *jong gūn*
mail *v* 郵寄 *yàuh gei*; *n* 郵件 *yàuh gín*
mailbox 郵箱 *yàuh sēung*
main attraction 主要景點 *jyú yiu gíng dím*
main course 主菜 *jyú choi*
make up *v* **[BE] (a prescription)** 藥方 *yeuhk fōng*
mall 購物中心 *kau maht jūng sām*
man 男人 *nàahm yán*
manager 經理 *gīng léih*
manicure 修手甲 *sāu sáu gaap*
manual car 手動汽車 *sáu duhng hei chē*
map 地圖 *deih tòuh*
market 市場 *síh chèuhng*
married 結咗婚 *git jó fān*

marry v 結婚 *git fān*

mass (church service) 禮拜 *láih baai*

massage 按摩 *ngon mō*

match n 火柴 *fó chàaih*

meal 飯 *faahn*

measure v **(someone)** 測量 *chāak leuhng*

measuring cup 量杯 *lèuhng būi*

measuring spoon 量羹 *lèuhng gāng*

mechanic 技工 *geih gūng*

medicine 醫藥 *yī yeuhk*

medium (size) 中等 *jūng dáng*

meet v **(someone)** 見面 *gin mihn*

meeting 會議 *wuih yíh*

meeting room 會議室 *wuih yíh sāt*

membership card 會員證 *wúih yùhn jing*

memorial (place) 紀念館 *gei nihm gún*

memory card 存儲卡 *chyúh chyùhn kāat*

mend v 修理 *sāu léih*

menstrual cramp 經期腹痛 *gīng kèih fūk tung*

menu 菜單 *choi dāan*

message 信息 *seun sīk*

microwave 微波爐 *mèih bō lòuh*

midday [BE] 晏晝 *ngaan jau*

midnight 午夜 *ngh yeh*

mileage 里數 *léih sou*

mini-bar 小酒吧 *síu jáu bā*

minute 分鐘 *fān jūng*

missing 錯過 *cho gwo*

mistake 差錯 *chā cho*

mobile phone [BE] 手提電話 *sáu tàih dihn wá*

mobility 流動性 *làuh dung sing*

monastery 修道院 *sāu douh yún*

money 錢 *chín*

month 月 *yuht piu*

mop 擦 *chaat*

moped 電單車 *dihn dāan chē*

more 多啲 *dō dī*

morning 早晨 *jóu sàhn*

mosque 清真寺 *chīng jān jí*

mother 媽媽 *màh mā*

motion sickness 暈浪 *wàhn lohng*

motor boat 汽船 *hei syùhn*

motorcycle 電單車 *dihn dāan chē*

motorway [BE] 高速公路 *gōu chūk gūng louh*

mountain 山 *sāan*

mountain bike 爬山電單車 *pàh sāan dihn dāan chē*

mouth 口 *háu*

movie 電影 *dihn yíng*

movie theater 電影院 *dihn yíng yún*

mug v 搶 *chéung*

multiple-trip (ticket) 無限次使用嘅 *mòuh haahn chi sí yuhng ge*

muscle 肌肉 *gēi yuhk*

museum 博物館 *bok maht gún*

music 音樂 *yām ngohk*

music store 音樂商店 *yām ngohk sēung dim*

N

nail file 指甲銼 *jí gaap cho*

name 名 *méng*

napkin 餐巾 *chāan gān*

nappy [BE] 尿片 *niuh pín*

nationality 國籍 *gwok jihk*

nature preserve 自然保護區 *jih yìhn bóu wuh kēui*

nauseous 想嘔 *séung ngáu*

near 附近 *fuh gahn*

near-sighted [BE] 近視 *gahn sih*

nearby 附近 *fuh gahn*

neck 頸 *géng*

necklace 頸鏈 *géng lín*

need v 需要 *sēui yiu*

newspaper 報紙 *bou jí*

newsstand 報攤 *bou tāan*

next 下一個 *hah yāt go*

nice 好 *hóu*

night 夜 *yeh*

nightclub 夜總會 *yeh júng wúi*

no 唔 *m*

non-alcoholic 無酒精 *mòuh jáu jīng*

non-smoking 禁煙 *gam yīn*

noon 中午 *jūng bouh*

north 北部 *bāk bouh*

nose 鼻 *beih*

nothing 冇乜野 *móuh māt yéh*

notify v 通知 *tūng jī*

novice (skill level) 新手 *sān sáu*

now 宜家 *yìh gā*

number 數字 *sou jih*

nurse 護士 *wuh sih*

O

office 辦公室 *baahn gūng sāt*

office hours 辦公時間 *baahn gūng sìh gaan*

off-license [BE] 酒店 *jáu dim*

oil 油 *yàuh*

OK 好 *hóu*

old 老 *lóuh*

one-way (ticket) 單程 *dāan chìhng*

one-way street 單程路 *dāan chìhng louh*

only 只係 *jí haih*

open v 打開 *dá hōi*; adj 開著 *hōi jeuhk*

opera 歌劇 *gō kehk*

opera house 歌劇院 *gō kehk yún*

opposite 相反 *sēung fáan*

optician 驗光師 *yihm gwōng sī*

orange (color) 橙 *cháng*

orchestra 管弦樂 *gún yìhng ngohk*

order *v* 叫野 *giu yéh*

outdoor pool 室外游泳池 *sāt ngoih yàuh wihng chìh*

outside 外面 *ngoih mihn*

overdone 太熟 *taai suhk*

overlook (scenic place) 俯視 *fú sih*

overnight 隔夜 *gaahk yeh*

oxygen treatment 氧氣治療 *yéuhng hei jih lìuh*

P

p.m. 下晝 *hah jau*

pacifier 奶嘴 *náaih jéui*

pack *v* 打包 *dá bāau*

package 包裹 *bāau gwó*

paddling pool [BE] 兒童泳池 *yìh tùhng wihng chìh*

pad [BE] (sanitary) 墊 *jin*

pain 痛 *tung*

pajamas 睡衣 *seuih yī*

palace 宮殿 *gūng dihn*

pants 褲 *fu*

pantyhose 絲襪 *sī maht*

paper 紙 *jí*

paper towel 紙巾 *jí gān*

park *v* 停車 *tìhng chē*; *n* 公園 *gūng yún*

parking garage 車房 *chē fòhng*

parking lot 停車場 *tìhng chē chèuhng*

parking meter 停車計時器 *tìhng chē gai sìh hei*

part-time 兼職 *gīm jīk*

passenger 乘客 *sìhng haak*

passport 護照 *wuh jiu*

passport control 護照管制 *wuh jiu gún jai*

password 密碼 *maht máh*

pastry shop 點心店 *dím sām dim*

path 道路 *douh louh*

pay *v* 支付 *jī fuh*

pay phone 公用電話 *gūng yuhng dihn wá*

peak (of a mountain) 山頂 *sāan déng*

pearl 珍珠 *jān jyū*

pedestrian 行人 *hàahng yàhn*

pediatrician 兒科醫生 *yìh fō yī sāng*

pedicure 修腳趾甲 *sāu jín geuk gaap*

pen 筆 *bāt*

per 每 *múih*

per day 每日 *múih yaht*

per hour 每個鐘頭 *múih go jūng tàuh*

per night 每晚 *múih máahn*

per week 每個星期 *múih go*

sīng kèih

perfume 香水 *hēung séui*

period (menstrual) 月經 *yuht gīng;* **(of time)** 期間 *kèih gāan*

permit *v* 准 *jéun*

petite 嬌小 *gīu síu*

petrol [BE] 汽油 *hei yàuh*

petrol station [BE] 加油站 *gā yàuh jaahm*

pharmacy 藥房 *yeuhk fòhng*

phone *v* 打電話 *dá dihn wá; n* 電話 *dihn wá*

phone call 電話 *dihn wá*

phone card 電話卡 *dihn wá kāat*

phone number 電話號碼 *dihn wá houh máh*

photo 相 *séung*

photocopy 影印本 *yíng yan bún*

photography 影相 *yíng séung*

picnic area 野餐區 *yéh chāan kēui*

piece 塊 *faai*

pill (birth control) 避孕丸 *beih yahn yún*

pillow 枕頭 *jám tàuh*

personal identification number (PIN) 個人密碼 *go yàhn maht máh*

pink 粉紅色 *fán hùhng sīk*

piste [BE] 小路 *síu louh*

piste map [BE] 小路路線圖 *síu louh louh sin tòuh*

place *v* **(a bet)** 落 *lohk*

plane 飛機 *fēi gēi*

plastic wrap 塑膠包裝 *sou gāau bāau jōng*

plate 碟 *díp*

platform 月臺 *yuht tòih*

platinum 鉑金 *baahk gām*

play *v* 玩 *wáan; n* **(theater)** 戲劇 *hei kehk*

playground 操場 *chōu chèuhng*

playpen 遊戲圍欄 *yàuh hei wàih làahn*

please 唔該 *m gōi*

pleasure 樂趣 *lohk cheui*

plunger 泵 *bām*

plus size 加大碼 *gā daaih máh*

pocket 袋 *dói*

poison 毒藥 *duhk yeuhk*

police 警察 *gíng chaat*

police report 警察報告 *gíng chaat bou gou*

police station 警察局 *gíng chaat gúk*

pond 池塘 *chìh tóng*

pool 水池 *séui chìh*

portion 部分 *bouh fahn*

post [BE] 郵件 *yàuh gín*

post office 郵局 *yàuh gúk*

postbox [BE] 郵箱 *yàuh sēung*

postcard 明信片 *mìhn seun pín*

pot 罐 *gun*

pottery 陶器 *tòuh hei*

pound (weight) 磅 *bohng*

pound (British sterling) 英鎊 *yīng bóng*

pregnant 有咗 *yáuh jó*

prescribe *v* 開處方 *hōi chyúh fōng*

prescription 處方藥 *chyúh fōng yeuhk*

press *v* (clothing) 熨 *tong*

price 價格 *ga gaak*

print *v* 列印 *liht yan*

problem 問題 *mahn tàih*

produce 農產品 *nùhng cháan bán*

produce store 農產品商店 *nùhng cháan bán sēung dim*

prohibit *v* 禁止 *gam jí*

pronounce *v* 發音 *faat yām*

public 公共 *gūng guhng*

pull *v* 拉 *lāai*

purple 紫色 *jí sīk*

purse 銀包 *ngàhn bāau*

push *v* 按 *ngon*

pushchair [BE] BB車 *bìhbī chē*

Q

quality 質量 *jāt leuhng*

question 問題 *mahn tàih*

quiet 安靜 *ngōn jihng*

R

racetrack 跑馬場 *páau máh chèuhng*

racket (sports) 球拍 *kàuh páak*

railway station [BE] 火車 *fó chē*

rain 雨 *yúh*

raincoat 雨褸 *yúh lāu*

rainforest 雨林 *yúh làhm*

rainy 多雨 *dō yúh*

rap (music) 說唱樂 *syut cheung lohk*

rape 強姦 *kèuhng gāan*

rare (object) 罕見 *hón gin*

rash 疹 *chán*

ravine 峽谷 *haap gūk*

razor blade 剃鬚刀 *tai sōu dōu*

reach *v* 到 *dou*

ready 準備好 *jéun beih hóu*

real 真正 *jān jing*

receipt 收據 *sāu geui*

receive *v* 接受 *jip sauh*

reception 招待會 *jīu doih wúi*

recharge *v* 充電 *chūng dihn*

recommend *v* 介紹 *gaai siuh*

recommendation 推薦 *tēui jin*

recycling 回收 *wùih sāu*

red 紅色 *hùhng sīk*

refrigerator 冰箱 *bīng sēung*

region 區域 *kēui wihk*

registered mail 掛號信 *gwa houh seun*

regular 普通 *pōu tūng*

relationship 關係 *gwāan haih*

Ren Min Bi (Chinese currency) 人民幣 *yàhn màhn baih*

rent v 租 *jōu*

rental car 的士 *dīk sí*

repair v 修理 *sāu léih*

repeat v 重複 *chùhng fūk*

reservation 預定 *yuh dihng*

reservation desk 服務台 *fuhk mouh tòih*

reserve v 預定 *yuh dehng*

restaurant 餐館 *chāan gún*

restroom 休息室 *yāu sīk sāt*

retired 退休 *teui yāu*

return v 還 *wàahn*

return (ticket) 雙程 *sēung chìhng*

reverse v **(the charges) [BE]** 對方付費電話 *deui fōng fuh fai dihn wá*

rib (body part) 肋骨 *laahk gwāt*

rice cooker 電飯煲 *dihn faahn bōu*

right of way 路權 *louh kyùhn*

ring 戒指 *gaai jí*

river 河 *hòh*

road map 路線圖 *louh sin tòuh*

roast v 烤 *hāau*

rob v 搶奪 *chéung dyuht*

robbed 畀人搶野 *béi yàhn chéung yéh*

romantic 浪漫 *lohng maahn*

room 房間 *fòhng gāan*

room key 房間鎖匙 *fòhng gāan só sìh*

room service 客房送餐服務 *haak fóng sung chāan fuhk mouh*

round-trip 雙程 *sēung chìhng*

route 路線 *louh sin*

rowboat 扒艇 *pàh téhng*

rubbish [BE] 垃圾 *laahp saap*

rubbish bag [BE] 垃圾袋 *laahp saap dói*

ruins 廢墟 *fai hēui*

rush 趕時間 *gón sìh gaan*

S

sad 傷心 *sēung sām*

safe (storage) 保險箱 *bóu hím sēung;* **(protected)** 安全 *ngōn chyùhn*

sales tax 銷售稅 *sīu sauh seui*

same 同一 *tùhng yāt*

sandals 涼鞋 *lèuhng hàaih*

sanitary napkin 衛生棉 *waih sāng mìhn*

saucepan 平底鑊 *pìhng dái wohk*

sauna 桑拿 *sōng nàh*

save v **(on a computer)** 保存 *bóu chyùhn*

savings (account) 儲蓄 *chyúh chūk*

scanner 掃描器 *sou mìuh hei*

scarf 絲巾 *sī gān*

schedule v 預定日程 *yuh dihng yaht chìhng;* n 日程表 *syaht chìhng bíu*

school 學校 *hohk haauh*

scissors 較剪 *gaau jín*

sea 海 *hói*

seat 座位 *joh wái*

security 保安 *bóu ngōn*

see v 睇見 *tái gin*

self-service 自助 *jih joh*

sell v 賣 *maaih*

seminar 研討會 *yìhng tóu wúi*

send v 送 *sung*

senior citizen 老年人 *lóuh nìhn yàhn*

separated (marriage) 分居 *fān gēui*

serious 嚴肅 *yìhm sūk*

service (in a restaurant) 服務 *fuhk mouh*

shampoo 洗頭水 *sái tàuh séui*

sharp 利 *leih*

shaving cream 剃鬚膏 *tai sōu gōu*

sheet 床單 *chòhng dāan*

ship v (mail) 運送 *wahn sung*

shirt 恤衫 *sēut sāam*

shoe store 鞋鋪 *hàaih póu*

shoes 鞋 *hàaih*

shop v 買野 *máaih yéh*

shopping 購物 *kau maht*

shopping area 購物區 *kau maht kēui*

shopping centre [BE] 商場 *sēung chèuhng*

shopping mall 商場 *sēung chèuhng*

short 短 *dyún*

short sleeves 短袖 *dyún jauh*

shorts 短褲 *dyún fu*

short-sighted [BE] 近視 *gahn sih*

shoulder 膊頭 *bok tàuh*

show v 顯示 *hín sih*

shower 沖涼 *chūng lèuhng*

shrine 寺廟 *jih míu*

sick 病 *behng*

side dish 配菜 *pui choi*

side effect 副作用 *fu jok yuhng*

sightseeing 觀光 *gūn gwōng*

sightseeing tour 觀光旅遊 *gūn gwōng léuih yàuh*

sign v 簽名 *chīm méng*

silk 絲綢 *sī chàuh*

silver 銀 *ngàhn*

single (unmarried) 單身 *dāan sān*

single bed 單人床 *dāan yàhn chòhng*

single room 單人房間 *dāan yàhn fóng*

sink 瓷盆 *chìh pùhn*

sister 姐妹 *jí múi*

sit v 坐低 *chóh dāi*

size 尺寸 *chek chyun*

skin 皮膚 *pèih fū*

skirt 裙 *kwàhn*

sleep *v* 訓覺 *fan gaau*

sleeper car 臥鋪車 *ngoh pōu chē*

sleeping bag 睡袋 *seuih dói*

sleeping car [BE] 臥鋪車 *ngoh pōu chē*

slice (of something) 片 *pin*

slippers 拖鞋 *tō háai*

slowly 慢慢地 *maahn máan déi*

small 小 *síu*

smoke *v* 食煙 *sihk yīn*

smoking (area) 食煙 *sihk yīn*

snack bar 小食店 *síu sihk dim*

sneaker 運動鞋 *wahn duhn hàaih*

snorkeling equipment 水底呼吸設備 *séui dái fū kāp chit beih*

soap 番鹼 *fāan gáan*

soccer 足球 *jūk kàuh*

sock 襪 *maht*

soother [BE] 奶嘴 *náaih jéui*

sore throat 喉嚨痛 *hàuh lùhng tung*

sorry 抱歉 *póu hip*

south 南 *nàahm*

souvenir 紀念品 *gei nihm bán*

souvenir store 紀念品商店 *gei nihm bán sēung dim*

spa 溫泉 *wān chyùhn*

spatula 鏟 *cháan*

speak *v* 講 *góng*

specialist (doctor) 專家 *jyūn gā*

specimen 標本 *bīu bún*

speeding 超速 *chīu chūk*

spell *v* 串 *chyun*

spicy 辣 *laaht*

spine (body part) 脊椎 *bui jēui*

spoon 匙羹 *chìh gāng*

sports 體育 *tái yuhk*

sporting goods store 體育用品商店 *tái yuhk yuhng bán sēung dim*

sports massage 按摩 *ngon mō*

sprain 扭傷 *náu sēung*

stadium 體育場 *tái yuhk chèuhng*

stairs 樓梯 *làuh tāi*

stamp *v* (a ticket) 蓋印 *koi yan; n* (postage) 郵票 *yàuh piu*

start *v* 開始 *hōi chíh*

starter [BE] 開胃菜 *hōi waih choi*

station 站 *jaahm*

statue 雕像 *dīu jeuhng*

stay *v* 住喺 *jyuh hái*

steal *v* 偷 *tāu*

steamer 蒸鍋 *jīng wō*

steep 斜 *che*

sterling silver 純銀 *syùhn ngán*

stewed 燉 *dahn*

stolen 畀人偷咗 *béi yàhn tāu jó*

stomach 胃 *waih*

stomachache 胃痛 *waih tung*

stop v 停低 *tìhng dāi*; n 站 *jaahm*

store directory 商店目錄 *sēung dim muhk luhk*

storey [BE] 層 *chàhng*

stove 爐 *lòuh*

straight 直 *jihk*

strange 奇怪 *kèih gwaai*

stream 小溪 *síu kāi*

stroller BB 車 *bìh bī chē*

student 學生 *hohk sāang*

study v 學習 *hohk jaahp*

stunning 震驚 *jan gīng*

subtitle 副標題 *fu bīu tàih*

subway 地鐵 *deih tit*

subway station 地鐵站 *deih tit jaahm*

suit 西服套裝 *sāi fuhk tou jōng*

suitcase 手提箱 *sáu tàih sēung*

sun 太陽 *taai yèuhng*

sunblock 防曬霜 *fòhng saai sēung*

sunburn 曬傷 *saai sēung*

sunglasses 太陽眼鏡 *taai yèuhng ngáahn géng*

sunny 晴朗 *chìhng lóhng*

sunscreen 防曬霜 *fòhng saai sēung*

sunstroke 中暑 *jung syú*

super (fuel) 超級 *chīu kāp*

supermarket 超級市場 *chīu kāp síh chèuhng*

supervision 監督 *gāam dzenask*

surfboard 滑浪板 *waaht lohng báan*

swallow v 吞 *tān*

sweater 毛衣 *mòuh yī*

sweatshirt 運動衫 *wahn duhng sāam*

sweet (taste) 甜 *tìhm*

swelling 腫 *júng*

swim v 游水 *yàuh séui*

swimsuit 泳衣 *wihng yī*

symbol (keyboard) 標誌 *bīu ji*

synagogue 猶太教堂 *yàuh taai gaau tóng*

T

table 檯 *tói*

tablet (medicine) 藥丸 *yeuhk yún*

take v 食藥 *sihk yeuhk*

take away [BE] 攞走 *ló jáu*

tampon 棉條 *mìhn tíu*

taste v 試吓 *si háh*

taxi 的士 *dīk sí*

team 隊 *déui*

teahouse 茶樓 *chàh làuh*

teaspoon 茶匙 *chàh chìh*

telephone 電話 *dihn wá*

temple (religious) 寺廟 *jíh míu*

temporary 臨時 *làhm sìh*

tennis 網球 *móhng kàuh*

tent 帳篷 *jeung fùhng*

tent peg 帳蓬椿 *jeung fùhng jōng*

tent pole 帳篷杆 *jeung fùhng gōn*

terminal (airport) 候機大堂 *hauh gēi daaih tòhng*

terrible 可怕 *hó pa*

text *v* **(send a message)** 發短信 *faat dyún seun; n* **(message)** 文字 *màhn jih*

thank *v* 感謝 *gám jeh*

thank you 多謝 *dō jeh*

that 嗰 *gó*

theater 戲院 *hei yún*

theft 偷竊 *tāu sit*

there 嗰度 *gó douh*

thief 賊 *cháak*

thigh 大腿 *daaih téui*

thirsty 口渴 *háu hot*

this 呢 *nī*

throat 喉嚨 *hàuh lùhng*

thunderstorm 雷雨 *lèuih yúh*

ticket 票 *piu*

ticket office 售票處 *sauh piu chyu*

tie (clothing) 領呔 *léhng tāai*

tights [BE] 絲襪 *sī maht*

time 時間 *sìh gaan*

timetable [BE] 時間表 *sìh gaan bíu*

tire 車胎 *chē tāai*

tired 癐喇 *guih la*

tissue 紙巾 *jí gān*

to go 去 *heui*

tobacconist 煙草零售商 *yīn chóu lìhng sauh sēung*

today 今日 *gām yaht*

toe 腳趾 *geuk jí*

toenail 趾甲 *jí gaap*

toilet [BE] 沖涼房 *chūng lèuhng fóng*

toilet paper 廁紙 *chi jí*

tomorrow 聽日 *tīng yaht*

tongue 舌 *siht*

tonight 今晚 *gām máahn*

too 太 *taai*

tooth 牙 *ngàh*

toothpaste 牙膏 *ngàh gōu*

total (amount) 一共 *yāt guhng*

tourist 旅客 *léuih haak*

tourist information office 旅遊資訊辦公室 *léuih yàuh jī seun baahn gūng sāt*

tour 遊覽 *yàuh láahm*

tow truck 拖車 *tō chē*

towel 毛巾 *mòuh gān*

tower 塔 *taap*

town 鎮 *jan*

town hall 市政廳 *síh jing tēng*

town map 市地圖 *síh deih tòuh*

town square 市中心廣場 *síh jūng sām gwóng chèuhng*

toy 玩具 *wuhn geuih*

toy store 玩具店 *wuhn geui dim*

track (train) 鐵軌 *tit gwái*

traditional 傳統 *chyùhn túng*

traffic light 紅綠燈 *hùhng luhk dāng*

trail 山路小徑 *sāan louh síu ging*

trail map 山路圖 *sāan louh tòuh*

train 火車 *fó chē*

train station 火車站 *fó chē jaahm*

transfer v (change trains/flights) 轉 *jyun*; v (money) 轉賬 *jyún jeung*

translate v 翻譯 *fāan yihk*

trash 垃圾 *laahp saap*

travel agency 旅行社 *léuih hàhng séh*

travel sickness 暈浪 *wàhn lohng*

traveler's check 旅行支票 *léuih hàhng jī piu*

traveller's cheque [BE] 旅行支票 *léuih hàhng jī piu*

tree 樹 *syuh*

trim (hair cut) 剪 *jín*

trip 旅程 *léuih chìhng*

trolley [BE] 電車 *dihn chē*

trousers [BE] 長褲 *chèuhng fu*

T-shirt T恤 *tī sēut*

turn off (lights) 熄 *sīk*

turn on (lights) 開 *hōi*

TV 電視 *dihn sih*

type v 打字 *dá jih*

U

ugly 難睇 *nàahn tái*

umbrella 遮 *jē*

unattended 無人睇 *móuh yàhn tái*

unconscious 冇知覺 *móuh jī gok*

underground [BE] 地下 *deih há*

underground station [BE] 地鐵站 *deih tit jaahm*

understand v 理解 *léih gáai*

underwear 底衫 *dái sāam*

unemployed 失業者 *sāt yihp jé*

United Kingdom (U.K.) 英國 *yīng gwok*

United States (U.S.) 美國 *méih gwok*

university 大學 *daaih hohk*

unleaded (gas) 無鉛 *mòuh yùnn*

upper 上部 *seuhng bouh*

upset stomach 腸胃不適 *chèuhng waih bāt sīk*

urgent 緊急 *gán gāp*

urine 尿 *niuh*

use v 使用 *sí yuhng*

username 用戶名 *yuhng wuh méng*

utensil 器皿 *hei míhng*

V

vacancy 有空房 *yáuh hūng fóng*

vacation 假期 *ga kèih*

vaccination 防疫 *fòhng yihk*

vacuum cleaner 吸塵器 *kāp chàhn hei*

vagina 陰道 *yām douh*

vaginal infection 陰道傳染 *yām douh chyùhn yíhm*

valid 合法 *hahp faat*

valley 河谷 *hòh gūk*

valuable 貴重嘅 *gwai juhng ge*

value 價值 *ga jihk*

vegetarian 素食者 *sou sihk jé*

vehicle registration 車輛註冊 *chē léuhng jyu chaak*

viewpoint [BE] 觀點 *gūn dím*

village 村莊 *chyūn jōng*

vineyard 葡萄園 *pòuh tòuh yùhn*

visa 簽證 *chīm jing*

visit v 參觀 *chāam gūn*

visiting hours 探病時間 *taam behng sìh gaan*

visually impaired 弱視者 *yeuhk sih j*

vitamin 維生素 *wàih sāng sou*

V-neck V 領 *wī léhng*

volleyball game 排球賽 *pàaih kàuh choi*

vomit v 嘔 *ngáu*

W

wait v 等 *dáng; n* 等候時間 *dáng hauh sìh gaan*

waiter 服務員 *fuhk mouh yùhn*

waiting room 候診室 *hauh chán āt*

waitress 女服務員 *néuih fuhk mouh yùhn*

wake v 醒 *séng*

wake-up call 叫醒服務 *giu séng fuhk mouh*

walk v 走 *jáu; n* 步行 *bouh hàhng*

walking route 步行路線 *bouh hàhng louh sin*

wall clock 掛鐘 *gwa jūng*

wallet 銀包 *ngàhn bāau*

war memorial 戰爭紀念館 *jin jāng gei nihm gún*

warm *adj/v* 暖 *nyúhn*

washing machine 洗衣機 *sái yī gēi*

watch 手錶 *sáu bīu*

water skis 滑水板 *waaht séui báan*

waterfall 瀑布 *bohk bou*

weather 天氣 *tīn hei*

week 星期 *sīng kèih*

weekend 週末 *jāu muht*

weekly 每週 *múih jāu*

welcome v 歡迎 *fūn yìhng*

well-rested 休息得好好 *yāu sīk dāk hóu hóu*

west 西部 *sāi bouh*

what 乜野 *māt yéh*

wheelchair 輪椅 *lèuhn yí*

wheelchair ramp 輪椅道 *lèuhn yí douh*
when 幾時 *géi sìh*
where 邊度 *bīn douh*
white 白色 *baahk sīk*
who 邊個 *bīn go*
wife 老婆 *lóuh pòh*
window 窗 *chēung*
window case 櫥窗 *chyùhn chēung*
wine list 酒類表 *jáu leuih bíu*
wireless internet 無線互聯網 *mòuh sin wuh lyùhn móhng*
wireless internet service 無線互聯網服務 *mòuh sin wuh lyùhn móhng fuhk mouh*
wireless phone 無線電話 *mòuh sin dihn wá*
with 同 *tùhng*
withdraw *v* 退出 *teui chēut*
withdrawal (bank) 取錢 *chéui chín*

without 冇 *móuh*
wok 炒鍋 *sō wō*
woman 女人 *néuih yán*
wool 羊毛 *yèuhng mòuh*
work *v* 做野 *jouh yéh*
wrap *v* **(a package)** 包 *bāau*
wrist 手腕 *sáu wún*
write *v* 寫 *sé*

Y

year 年 *nìhn*
yellow 黃色 *wòhng sīk*
yes 係 *haih*
yesterday 琴日 *kàhm yaht*
young 年輕 *nìhn hīng*
youth hostel 青年旅舍 *chīng nìhn léuih se*

Z

zoo 動物園 *duhng maht yùhn*

A

阿斯匹零 **a sī pāt lìhng** aspirin

B

芭蕾 **bā lèuih** ballet

巴士 **bā sí** bus

巴士車票 **bā sí chē piu** bus ticket

巴士站 **bā sí jaahm** bus station; bus stop

巴士遊覽 **bā sí yàuh láahm** bus tour

鉑金 **baahk gām** platinum

白色 **baahk sīk** white

辦公室 **baahn gūng sāt** office

辦公時間 **baahn gūng sìh gaan** office hours

辦理登機手續 **baahn léih dāng gēi sáu juhk** check-in (airport)

百貨公司 **baak fo gūng sī** department store

包 **bāau** v wrap (a package)

包裹 **bāau gwó** package

包括 **bāau kwut** v include

北部 **bāk bouh** north

泵 **bām** plunger

繃帶 **bāng dáai** bandage

筆 **bāt** pen

病 **behng** sick [ill BE]

畀 **béi** v give

比較少 **béi gaau síu** less

比基尼裝 **béi gīn nèih jōng** bikini

畀人搶野 **béi yàhn chéung yéh** robbed

畀人偷咗 **béi yàhn tāu jó** stolen

鼻 **beih** nose

避孕丸 **beih yahn yún** pill (birth control)

避孕套 **beih yan tou** condom

BB **bìh bī** baby

BB車 **bìhbī chē** stroller [pushchair BE]

邊度 **bīn douh** where

邊個 **bīn go** who

便秘 **bin bei** constipated

變壓器 **bin ngaat hei** adapter

冰 **bīng** ice

冰球 **bīng kàuh** ice hockey

冰冷 **bīng láahng** icy

冰箱 **bīng sēung** refrigerator

標本 **bīu bún** specimen

表格 **bíu gaak** form (fill-in)

標誌 **bīu ji** symbol (keyboard)

玻璃 **bō lēi** glass (material)

玻璃杯 **bō lēi būi** glass (drinking)

瀑布 **bohk bou** waterfall
磅 **bohng** pound (weight)
博物館 **bok maht gún** museum
膊頭 **bok tàuh** shoulder
幫助 **bōng joh** help
保存 **bóu chyùhn** v save (on a computer)
保險 **bóu hím** insurance
保險公司 **bóu hím gūng sī** insurance company
保險卡 **bóu hím kāat** insurance card
保險箱 **bóu hím sēung** safe (storage)
保姆 **bóu móuh** babysitter
保安 **bóu ngōn** security
保鮮紙 **bóu sīn jí** plastic wrap [cling film BE]
報紙 **bou jí** newspaper
報攤 **bou tāan** newsstand
部分 **bouh fahn** portion
曝光 **bouh gwōng** exposure (film)
步行 **bouh hàhng** n walk
步行路線 **bouh hàhng louh sin** walking route
撥號 **buht houh** v dial
杯 **būi** cup
背脊 **bui jek** back (body part)
脊椎 **bui jēui** spine (body part)
背囊 **bui nòhng** backpack
背痛 **bui tung** backache

半 **bun** half
半公斤 **bun gūng gān** half-kilo
半小時 **bun síu sìh** half hour

C

叉 **chā** fork
差錯 **chā cho** mistake
殘疾 **chàahn jaht** disabled; handicapped
殘疾人通道 **chàahn jaht yàhn tūng douh** hadicapped [disabled BE] accessible
踩單車 **cháai dāan chē** cycling
賊 **cháak** thief
測量 **chāak leuhng** v measure (someone)
參觀 **chāam gūn** v visit
鏟 **cháan** spatula
餐巾 **chāan gān** napkin
餐館 **chāan gún** restaurant
橙 **cháang** orange (color)
插入 **chaap yahp** v insert (on an ATM)
擦 **chaat** mop
茶匙 **chàh chìh** teaspoon
茶樓 **chàh làuh** teahouse
陳列櫃 **chàhn liht gwaih** display case
柴油 **chàih yàuh** diesel
疹 **chán** rash
漆器 **chāt hei** lacquerware

斜 **che** steep

車房 **chē fòhng** parking garage

車輛註冊 **chē léuhng jyu chaak** vehicle registration

車胎 **chē tāai** tire [tyre BE]

尺寸 **chek chyun** size

長 **chèuhng** long

長褲 **chèuhng fu** pants [trousers BE]

長袖 **chèuhng jauh** long sleeves

長筒襪 **chèuhng túng maht** tight

腸胃不適 **chèuhng waih bāt sīk** upset stomach

錘 **chéui** hammer

取錢 **chéui chín** withdrawal (bank)

取消 **chéui sīu** v cancel

搶 **chéung** v mug

腸 **chéung** intestine

窗 **chēung** window

搶奪 **chéung dyuht** v rob

出口 **chēut háu** n exit

出去 **chēut heui** v exit

出席 **chēut jihk** v attend

出租汽車 **chēut jōu hei chē** car rental [hire BE]

出納員 **chēut naahp yùhn** cashier

廁紙 **chi jí** toilet paper

遲啲 **chìh dī** v delay

匙羹 **chìh gāng** spoon

瓷器 **chìh hei** china

遲咗 **chìh jó** late (time)

瓷盆 **chìh pùhn** sink

池塘 **chìh tóng** pond

潛水 **chìhm séui** v dive

潛水用具 **chìhm séui yuhng geuih** diving equipment

晴朗 **chìhng lóhng** sunny

簽證 **chīm jing** visa

簽名 **chīm méng** v sign

錢 **chín** money

清除 **chīng chèuih** v clear (on an ATM)

清潔產品 **chīng git cháan bán** cleaning product

清真寺 **chīng jān jí** mosque

清真食品 **chīng jān sihk bán** halal

青年旅舍 **chīng nìhn léuih se** youth hostel

設備 **chit beih** equipment

超速 **chīu chūk** speeding

超過 **chīu gwo** excess

超級 **chīu kāp** super (fuel)

超級市場 **chīu kāp síh chèuhng** supermarket

錯過 **cho gwo** missing

初學者 **chō hohk jé** beginner (skill level)

坐低 **chóh dāi** v sit

床 **chòhng** bed
床單 **chòhng dāan** sheet
床仔 **chòhng jái** cot
菜單 **choi dāan** menu
艙 **chōng** class
闖入 **chóng yahp** break-in (burglary)
操場 **chōu chèuhng** playground
蟲 **chùhng** bug
重複 **chùhng fūk** v repeat
蟲咬 **chùhng ngáau** insect bite
充電 **chūng dihn** v recharge
充血 **chūng hyut** congestion
沖涼 **chūng lèuhng** shower
櫥窗 **chyùh chēung** window case
儲蓄 **chyúh chūk** n deposit (bank); savings (account)
存儲卡 **chyúh chyùhn kāat** memory card
廚房 **chyùh fóng** kitchen
廚房錫紙 **chyùh fóng sehk jí** aluminum [kitchen BE] foil
處方藥 **chyúh fōng yeuhk** prescription
存錢 **chyùhn chín** v deposit
傳真 **chyùhn jān** n fax
傳真號碼 **chyùhn jān houh máh** fax number
傳統 **chyùhn túng** traditional
傳染 **chyùhn yíhm** infected
傳染嘅 **chyùhn yíhm ge** contagious
串 **chyun** v spell
村莊 **chyūn jōng** village

D

打包 **dá bāau** v pack
打電話 **dá dihn wá** v call;phone
打火機 **dá fó gēi** lighter
打攪 **dá gáau** v bother
打開 **dá hōi** v open
打字 **dá jih** v type
帶嚟 **daai làih** v bring
大 **daaih** large
大教堂 **daaih gaau tòhng** cathedral
大廈 **daaih hah** building
大學 **daaih hohk** university
大腿 **daaih tēui** thigh
單 **dāan** n bill (of sale)
單車 **dāan chē** bicycle
單車路線 **dāan chē louh sin** bike route
單程 **dāan chìhng** one-way (ticket)
單程路 **dāan chìhng louh** one-way street
單獨 **dāan duhk** alone
單身 **dāan sān** single (unmarried)
單人床 **dāan yàhn chòhng** single bed
單人房間 **dāan yàhn fóng**

single room

搭車 **daap chē** v hitchhike

燉 **dahn** stewed

低 **dāi** low

抵達 **dái daaht** arrivals (airport)

底衫 **dái sāam** underwear

第一 **daih yāt** first

得意 **dāk yi** cute

凳 **dang** chair

等 **dáng** v wait

燈 **dāng** light (overhead)

燈膽 **dāng dáam** lightbulb

登機 **dāng gēi** v board

登機証 **dāng gēi jing** boarding pass

登機門 **dāng gēi mùhn** gate [airport]

等候時間 **dáng hauh sìh gaan** n wait

登錄 **dāng luhk** log on

地板 **deih báan** floor

地址 **deih jí** address

地鐵 **deih tit** subway [underground BE]

地鐵站 **deih tit jaahm** subway station [underground BE]

地圖 **deih tòuh** map

隊 **déui** team

對方付費電話 **deui fōng fuh fai dihn wá** v call collect [reverse the charges BE]

兌換 **deui wuhn** v exchange (money)

兌換率 **deui wuhn léut** exchange rate

DVD **dī wī dī** DVD

滴 **dihk** drop (medicine)

電車 **dihn chē** tram

電單車 **dihn dāan chē** motorcycle

電飯煲 **dihn faahn bōu** rice cooker

電風扇 **dihn fūng sin** fan (appliance)

電制 **dihn jai** electric outlet

電子票 **dihn jí piu** e-ticket

電子郵件 **dihn jí yàuh gín** n e-mail

電腦 **dihn nóuh** computer

電芯 **dihn sām** battery

電視 **dihn sih** TV

電梯 **dihn tāi** lift [elevator BE]

電筒 **dihn túng** flashlight

電話 **dihn wá** n call; phone call; telephone

電話號碼 **dihn wá houh máh** phone number

電話卡 **dihn wá kāat** phone card

電郵地址 **dihn yàuh deih jí** e-mail address

電影 **dihn yíng** movie

電影院 **dihn yíng yún** movie

theater

碟 **dihp** dish (kitchen)

的士 **dīk sí** taxi

點 **dím** light (cigarette)

點心店 **dím sām dim** pastry
   shop

點樣 **dím yéung** how

癲癇 **dīn gáan** epileptic

碟 **díp** plate

雕刻 **dīu hāk** v engrave

雕像 **dīu jeuhng** statue

吊車 **diu chē** drag lift

多啲 **dō dī** more

多謝 **dō jeh** thank you

多雨 **dō yúh** rainy

袋 **dói** bag; pocket

代辦處 **doih baahn chyu** agency

當地 **dōng deih** local

刀 **dōu** knife

賭場 **dóu chèuhng** casino

倒空 **dóu hūng** v empty

到 **dou** get to; v reach

到達 **dou daaht** v arrive

度 **douh** degrees (temperature)

渡輪 **douh lèuhn** ferry

道路 **douh louh** path

導盲犬 **douh màahng hyún**
   guide dog

毒藥 **duhk yeuhk** poison

動脈 **duhng mahk** artery

動物 **duhng maht** animal

動物園 **duhng maht yùhn** zoo

東部 **dūng bouh** east

短 **dyún** short

短褲 **dyún fu** shorts

短袖 **dyún jauh** short sleeves

F

花 **fā** flower

化妝乳液 **fa jōng yúh yihk**
   lotion

飯 **faahn** meal

飯廳 **faahn tēng** dining room

快 **faai** express

塊 **faai** piece

快餐 **faai chāan** fast food

快速 **faai chūk** fast

筷子 **faai jí** chopsticks

番鹼 **fāan gáan** soap

翻譯 **fāan yihk** v translate

發傳真 **faat chyùhn jān** v fax

發電郵 **faat dihn yàuh** v e-mail

發短信 **faat dyún seun** v text
   (send a message)

發貨單 **faat fo dāan** invoice

琺瑯 **faat lòhng** enamel (jewelry)

髮廊 **faat lòhng** hair salon

發燒 **faat sīu** fever

發音 **faat yām** v pronounce

髮型 **faat yìhng** hairstyle

髮型師 **faat yìhng sī** hairstylist

罰款 **faht fún** fine (fee)

肺 **fai** lung

廢墟 **fai hēui** ruins

費用 **fai yuhng** fee

花粉症 **fān fán jing** hay fever

分機 **fān gēi** extension (phone)

分居 **fān gēui** separated (marriage)

分鐘 **fān jūng** minute

粉紅色 **fán hùhng sīk** pink

訓覺 **fan gaau** v sleep

飛髮 **fēi faat** haircut

飛機 **fēi gēi** airplane

飛機場 **fēi gēi chèuhng** airport

菲林 **fēi lám** film (camera)

火 **fó** fire

火柴 **fó chàaih** n match

火車 **fó chē** train

火車站 **fó chē jaahm** train [railway BE] station

貨幣 **fo baih** currency

貨幣兌換 **fo baih deui wuhn** currency exchange

貨幣兌換局 **fo baih deui wuhn gúk** currency exchange office

課程 **fo chìhng** lesson

防火門 **fòhng fó mùhn** fire door

房間 **fòhng gāan** room

房間鎖匙 **fòhng gāan só sìh** room key

防曬霜 **fòhng saai sēung** sunblock

防疫 **fòhng yihk** vaccination

方向 **fōng heung** direction

褲 **fu** pants

呼吸 **fū kāp** v breathe

俯視 **fú sih** overlook (scenic place)

副標題 **fu bīu tàih** subtitle

副作用 **fu jok yuhng** side effect

婦產科醫生 **fúh cháan fō yī sāng** gynecologist

父親 **fuh chān** father

附加費 **fuh gā fai** cover charge

附近 **fuh gahn** near; nearby

服裝要求 **fuhk jōng yīu kàuh** dress code

服務 **fuhk mouh** service (in a restaurant)

服務台 **fuhk mouh tòih** reservation desk

服務員 **fuhk mouh yùhn** waiter

灰色 **fūi sīk** gray

歡迎 **fūn yìhng** v welcome

風筒 **fūng túng** hair dryer

G

加大碼 **gā daaih máh** extra large

加滿 **gā múhn** v fill up (food)

家庭 **gā tìhng** family

加入 **gā yahp** v join

加油站 **gā yàuh jaahm** gas

[petrol BE] station
加熱 **gā yiht** heat
加熱器 **gā yiht hei** heater
假牙 **gá ngàh** denture
咖啡店 **ga fē dim** coffee shop
咖啡館 **ga fē gún** cafe
咖啡色 **ga fē sīk** brown
價格 **ga gaak** price
價格固定嘅菜單 **ga gaak gu dihng ge choi dāan** fixed-price menu
價值 **ga jihk** value
假期 **ga kèih** vacation [holiday BE]
加拿大 **ga nàh daaih** Canada
駕駛執照號碼 **ga sái jāp jiu houh máh** driver's license number
隔夜 **gaahk yeh** overnight
戒指 **gaai jí** ring
介紹 **gaai siuh** v introduce
監督 **gāam dūk** supervision
交換 **gāau wuhn** v exchange (goods)
較剪 **gaau jín** scissors
教堂 **gaau tóng** church
近視 **gahn sih** near-sighted [short-sighted BE]
計時器 **gai sìh hei** meter (parking)
金 **gām** gold
今晚 **gām máahn** tonight
感謝 **gám jeh** v thank

感冒 **gám mouh** cold (sickness)
今日 **gām yaht** today
禁止 **gam jí** v prohibit
禁煙 **gam yīn** non-smoking
緊急 **gán gāp** urgent
緊急出口 **gán gāp chēut háu** emergency exit
緊急狀態 **gán gāp johng taai** emergency
緊身褲 **gán sān fu** briefs (clothing)
更改路線 **gāng gói louh sin** alternate route
救生衣 **gau sāng yī** life jacket
救生員 **gau sāng yùhn** lifeguard
救護車 **gau sēung chē** ambulance
肌肉 **gēi yuhk** muscle
幾多 **géi dō** how much
幾時 **géi sìh** when
紀念品 **gei nihm bán** souvenir
紀念品商店 **gei nihm bán sēung dim** souvenir store
紀念館 **gei nihm gún** memorial (place)
技工 **geih gūng** mechanic
頸 **géng** neck
頸鏈 **géng lín** necklace
鏡片 **geng pín** lens
腳趾 **geui jí** toe
腳 **geuk** foot

腳眼 **geuk ngáahn** ankle

件 **gihn** case (amount)

健康 **gihn hōng** health

健康食品店 **gihn hōng sihk bán dim** health food store

檢查 **gím chàh** v check (something)

兼職 **gīm jīk** part-time

見面 **gin mihn** v meet (someone)

警察 **gíng chaat** police

警察報告 **gíng chaat bou gou** police report

警察局 **gíng chaat gúk** police station

經濟艙 **gīng jai chōng** economy class

經期腹痛 **gīng kèih fūk tung** menstrual cramp

經理 **gīng léih** manager

景泰藍 **gíng taai làahm** cloisonné

結束 **git chūk** v end

結婚 **git fān** v marry

嬌小 **gīu síu** petite

叫醒服務 **giu séng fuhk mouh** wake-up call

叫野 **giu yéh** v order

歌劇 **gō kehk** opera

歌劇院 **gō kehk yún** opera house

嗰 **gó** that

嗰度 **gó douh** there

個人密碼 **go yàhn maht máh** personal identification number (PIN)

改 **gói** v alter (clothing)

乾淨 **gōn jehng** adj clean

肝臟 **gōn johng** liver (body part)

乾洗店 **gōn sái dim** dry cleaner

趕時間 **gón sìh gaan** rush

講 **góng** v speak

港元 **góng yùhn** dollar (H.K.)

高 **gōu** high

高速公路 **gōu chūk gūng louh** highway [motorway BE]

高腳椅 **gōu geuk yí** highchair

高爾夫球比賽 **gōu yíh fū kàuh béi choi** golf tournament

高爾夫球場 **gōu yíh fū kàuh chèuhng** golf course

古典音樂 **gú dím yām ngohk** classical music

古董店 **gú dúng dim** antiques store

古龍水 **gú lùhng séui** cologne

故障 **gu jeung** breakdown

顧問 **gu mahn** consultant

雇用 **gu yuhng** v hire

瘤喇 **guih la** tired

罐 **gun** pot

觀點 **gūn dím** overlook [viewpoint BE]

觀光 **gūn gwōng** sightseeing

觀光旅遊 **gūn gwōng léuih yàuh** sightseeing tour

宮殿 **gūng dihn** palace

公斤 **gūng gān** kilogram

攻擊 **gūng gīk** attack (on person)

公共 **gūng guhng** public

公仔 **gūng jái** doll

公里 **gūng léih** kilometer

公升 **gūng sīng** liter

公寓 **gūng yuh** apartment

公用電話 **gūng yuhng dihn wá** pay phone

公園 **gūng yún** n park

掛號信 **gwa houh seun** registered mail

掛鐘 **gwa jūng** wall clock

關閉 **gwāan bai** closed

關係 **gwāan haih** relationship

關節 **gwāan jit** joint (body part)

關節炎 **gwāan jit yìhm** arthritis

關門 **gwāan mùhn** v close (a shop)

關稅 **gwāan seui** duty (tax)

貴重嘅 **gwai juhng ge** valuable

骨頭 **gwāt tàuh** bone

過敏反應 **gwo máhn fáan ying** allergic reaction

國家代號 **gwok gā doih houh** country code

國際 **gwok jai** international

(airport area)

國際學生證 **gwok jai hohk sāang jing** international student card

國際航班 **gwok jai hòhng bāan** international flight

國籍 **gwok jihk** nationality

國內 **gwok noih** domestic

國內航班 **gwok noih hòhng bāan** domestic flight

H

行人 **hàahng yàhn** pedestrian

鞋 **hàaih** shoes

鞋帶 **hàaih dáai** lace

鞋鋪 **hàaih póu** shoe store

客艙 **haak chōng** cabin

客房清潔服務 **haak fóng chīng git fuhk móuh** housekeeping services

客房送餐服務 **haak fóng sung chāan fuhk mouh** room service

峽谷 **haap gūk** ravine

烤 **hāau** v roast

烤肉 **hāau yuhk** barbecue

下晝 **hah jau** afternoon; p.m.

下爬 **hah pàh** jaw

下一個 **hah yāt go** next

行李 **hàhng léih** luggage

行李車 **hàhng léih chē** cart (luggage)

行李暫存箱 **hàhng léih jaahm chyùhn sēung** luggage locker

行李票 **hàhng léih piu** luggage [baggage BE] ticket

行李推車 **hàhng léih tēui chē** luggage cart [trolley BE]

行李認領 **hàhng léih yihng léhng** baggage claim

合法 **hahp faat** valid

喺 **hái** in

係 **haih** yes

克 **hāk** gram

黑暗 **hāk ngam** dark

黑色 **hāk sīk** black

口 **háu** mouth

口渴 **háu hot** thirsty

口譯員 **háu yihk yùhn** interpreter

喉嚨 **hàuh lùhng** throat

喉嚨痛 **hàuh lùhng tung** sore throat

候診室 **hauh chán sāt** waiting room

候機大堂 **hauh gēi daaih tòhng** terminal (airport)

後面 **hauh mihn** behind (direction)

起飛 **héi fēi** *v* leave

氣泵 **hei bām** air pump

汽車 **hei chē** car

汽車座位 **hei chē joh wái** car seat

氣喘 **hei chyún** asthmatic

戲劇 **hei kehk** *n* play (theater)

器皿 **hei míhng** utensil

汽船 **hei syùhn** motor boat

汽油 **hei yàuh** gasoline [petrol BE]

戲院 **hei yún** theater

靴 **hēu** boots

去 **heui** *v* go (somewhere)

香薰療法 **hēung fān liuh faat** aromatherapy

香口膠 **hēung háu gāau** chewing gum

香水 **hēung séui** perfume

享用 **héung yuhng** *v* enjoy

顯示 **hín sih** *v* show

兄弟 **hīng daih** brother

可怕 **hó pa** terrible

河 **hòh** river

河谷 **hòh gūk** valley

學校 **hohk haauh** school

學習 **hohk jaahp** *v* study

學生 **hohk sāang** student

航班 **hòhng bāan** flight

航空公司 **hòhng hūng gūng sī** airline

航空信 **hòhng hūng seun** airmail

開 **hōi** turn on (lights)

開車 **hōi chē** *v* drive

開始 **hōi chí** *v* begin; start
開處方 **hōi chyúh fōng** *v* prescribe
開單 **hōi dāan** *v* bill (charge)
開罐器 **hōi gun hei** can opener
海關 **hói gwāan** customs
開酒器 **hōi jáu hei** corkscrew
開著 **hōi jeuhk** *adj* open
開瓶器 **hōi pìhng hei** bottle opener
開胃菜 **hōi waih choi** appetizer [starter BE]
海 **hói** sea
海灘 **hói tāan** beach
罕見 **hón gin** rare (object)
好 **hóu** *adj* good
好食 **hóu sihk** delicious
紅綠燈 **hùhng luhk dāng** traffic light
紅色 **hùhng sīk** red
胸圍 **hūng wàih** bra
血壓 **hyut ngaat** blood pressure
血液 **hyut yihk** blood

J

碴 **jā** carafe; jar
站 **jaahm** station
雜貨店 **jaahp fo dim** grocery store
雜誌 **jaahp ji** magazine
針灸 **jām gau** acupuncture
枕頭 **jám tàuh** pillow
真正 **jān jing** real

珍珠 **jān jyū** pearl
鎮 **jan** town
震驚 **jan gīng** stunning
質量 **jāt leuhng** quality
週末 **jāu muht** weekend
走 **jáu** *v* walk
酒吧 **jáu bā** bar (place)
酒店 **jáu dim** hotel
酒類表 **jáu leuih bíu** wine list
遮 **jē** umbrella
借記卡 **je gei kāat** debit card
最後 **jeui hauh** last
最好 **jeui hóu** best
嘴唇 **jéui sèuhn** lip
雀仔 **jeuk jái** bird
爵士樂 **jeuk sih ngohk** jazz
爵士樂俱樂部 **jeuk sih ngohk kēui lohk bouh** jazz club
准 **jéun** *v* permit
樽 **jēun** bottle
準備好 **jéun beih hóu** ready
准許 **jéun héui** *v* allow
進入 **jeun yahp** *v* enter
帳篷 **jeung fùhng** tent
帳篷杆 **jeung fùhng gōn** tent pole
帳蓬樁 **jeung fùhng jōng** tent peg
帳戶 **jeung wuh** account
支付 **jī fuh** *v* pay
支票 **jī piu** check [cheque BE]

支票戶口 **jī piu wuh háu**
checking [current BE] account

紙 **jí** paper

紙幣 **jí baih** n bill (money)

指甲 **jí gaap** fingernail

趾甲 **jí gaap** toenail

指甲銼 **jí gaap cho** nail file

紙巾 **jí gān** paper towel; tissue

只係 **jí haih** only

止汗劑 **jí hon jāi** deodorant

姐妹 **jí múi** sister

指南 **jí nàahm** guide book

紫色 **jí sīk** purple

自動扶梯 **jih duhng fùh tāi**
escalator

自動提款機 **jih duhng tàih fún gēi** ATM

自動提款卡 **jih duhng tàih fún kāat** ATM card

自助 **jih joh** self-service

寺廟 **jíh míu** temple (religious)

自然保護區 **jih yìhn bóu wuh kēui** nature preserve

直 **jihk** straight

植物園 **jihk maht yùhn**
botanical garden

即棄 **jik hei** disposable

即棄剃鬚刀 **jīk hei tai sōu dōu**
disposable razor

即時訊息 **jīk sìh seun sīk**
instant message

毯 **jīn** blanket

煎鍋 **jīn wō** frying pan

剪 **jín** trim (hair cut)

戰場 **jin chèuhng** battleground

戰爭紀念館 **jin jāng gei nihm gún** war memorial

蒸鍋 **jīng wō** steamer

證件 **jing gín** identification

症狀 **jing johng** condition (medical)

證明 **jing mìhng** certificate

證實 **jing saht** v confirm

接受 **jip sauh** v accept

折 **jit** discount

招待會 **jīu doih wúi** reception

左邊 **jó bīn** left (direction)

座位 **joh wái** seat

撞 **johng** v crash (car)

再見 **joi gin** goodbye

壯觀 **jong gūn** magnificent

租 **jōu** v rent

租用汽車 **jōu yuhng hei chē**
rental [hire BE] car

早 **jóu** early

早餐 **jóu chāan** breakfast

祖父母 **jóu fuh móuh**
grandparent

早晨 **jóu sàhn** good morning

做 **jouh** v have

做野 **jouh yéh** v work

足球 **jūk kàuh** soccer [football BE]

中午 **jūng bouh** noon
中等 **jūng dáng** medium (size)
中國 **jūng gwok** China
中國畫 **jūng gwok wá** Chinese painting
中文 **jūng màhn** Chinese
鍾意 **jūng yi** v like
腫 **júng** swelling
中暑 **jung syú** sunstroke
珠寶商 **jyū bóu sēung** jeweler
主菜 **jyú choi** main course
主要景點 **jyú yiu gíng dím** main attraction
住 **jyuh** v live
住喺 **jyuh hái** v stay
住宿 **jyuh sūk** accommodation
專家 **jyūn gā** specialist (doctor)
轉賬 **jyún jeung** v transfer (money)
轉 **jyun** v transfer (change trains/flights)
轉機 **jyun gēi** connection (flight)
轉角處 **jyun gok chyu** around (the corner)
鑽石 **jyun sehk** diamond

K

卡路里 **kā louh léih** calories
卡 **kāat** card
咭片 **kāat pín** business card
琴日 **kàhm yaht** yesterday
近 **kahn** close
吸塵器 **kāp chàhn hei** vacuum cleaner
咳 **kāt** n/v cough
購物 **kau maht** shopping
購物中心 **kau maht jūng sām** shopping centre [mall BE]
購物區 **kau maht kēui** shopping area
購物籃 **kau maht láam** basket (grocery store)
球拍 **kàuh páak** racket (sports)
期間 **kèih gjāan** during; period (of time)
奇怪 **kèih gwaai** strange
強姦 **kèuhng gāan** rape
區號 **kēui houh** area code
俱樂部 **kēui lohk bouh** club
區域 **kēui wihk** region
拒絕 **kéuih jyuht** v decline (credit card)
橋樑 **kìuh lèuhng** bridge
蓋印 **koi yan** v stamp (a ticket)
抗生素 **kong sāng sou** antibiotic
曲棍球 **kūk gwan kàuh** hockey
裙 **kwàhn** skirt
困難 **kwan nàahn** difficult
拳擊比賽 **kyùhn gīk béi choi** boxing match

L

肋骨 **laahk gwāt** rib (body part)

籃球 **làahm kàuh** basketball

藍色 **làahm sīk** blue

爛 **laahn** v break (tooth)

爛咗 **laahn jó** broken

冷 **láahng** cold (temperature)

冷氣 **láahng hei** air conditioning

垃圾 **laahp saap** garbage [rubbish BE]

垃圾袋 **laahp saap dói** garbage [rubbish BE] bag

辣 **laaht** hot (spicy)

拉 **lāai** v pull

攬 **láam** v hug

臨時 **làhm sih** temporary

嚟 **làih** v come

禮拜 **láih baai** mass (church service)

禮品店 **láih bán dim** gift shop

禮服 **láih fuhk** dress (piece of clothing)

禮物 **láih maht** gift

褸 **lāu** jacket

流動性 **làuh dung sing** mobility

流行音樂 **làuh hàhng yām ngohk** pop music

流血 **làuh hyut** v bleed

樓梯 **làuh tāi** stairs

領呔 **léhng tāai** tie (clothing)

利 **leih** sharp

離婚 **lèih fān** v divorce

離開 **lèih hōi** departure

釐米 **lèih máih** centimeter

理髮師 **léih faat sī** barber

理解 **léih gáai** v understand

里數 **léih sou** mileage

靚 **leng** beautiful

輪椅 **lèuhn yí** wheelchair

輪椅道 **lèuhn yí douh** wheelchair ramp

涼 **lèuhng** cool (temperature)

量杯 **lèuhng būi** measuring cup

量羹 **lèuhng gāng** measuring spoon

涼鞋 **lèuhng hàaih** sandals

律師 **leuht sī** lawyer

雷雨 **lèuih yúh** thunderstorm

旅程 **léuih chìhng** trip

旅客 **léuih haak** tourist

旅行支票 **léuih hàhng jī piu** traveler's check [cheque BE]

旅行社 **léuih hàhng séh** travel agency

旅舍 **léuih se** hostel

旅遊資訊辦公室 **léuih yàuh jī seun baahn gūng sāt** tourist information office

連接 **lìhn jip** connection (internet); v connect (internet)

領事館 **líhng sih gún** consulate

令人驚奇嘅 **lihng yàhn gīng kèih ge** amazing

列印 **liht yan** *v* print

落 **lohk** *v* place (a bet)

落車 **lohk chē** get off (a train/bus/subway)

樂趣 **lohk cheui** pleasure

浪漫 **lohng maahn** romantic

爐 **lòuh** stove

老 **lóuh** old

老公 **lóuh gūng** husband

老年人 **lóuh nìhn yàhn** senior citizen

老婆 **lóuh pòh** wife

路口位 **louh háu wái** aisle seat

路權 **louh kyùhn** right of way

路線 **louh sin** route

路線圖 **louh sin tòuh** road map

露營 **louh yìhng** *v* camp

露營爐 **louh yìhng lòuh** camping stove

綠色 **luhk sīk** green

聾 **lùhng** deaf

聯繫 **lyùhn haih** *v* contact

M

唔 **m** no

唔見咗 **m gin jó** *v* lose (something)

唔該 **m gōi** please

唔貴 **m gwai** inexpensive

晚餐 **máahn chāan** dinner

晚安 **máahn ngōn** good evening

慢慢地 **maahn máan déi** slowly

盲腸 **màahng chéung** appendix (body part)

買 **máaih** *v* buy

買野 **máaih yéh** *v* shop

賣 **maaih** *v* sell

賣花人 **maaih fā yàhn** florist

麻布 **màh bou** linen

麻醉 **màh jeui** anesthesia

媽媽 **màh mā** mother

民間音樂 **màhn gāan yām ngohk** folk music

文字 **màhn jih** *n* text (message)

敏感 **máhn gám** allergic

問題 **mahn tàih** problem; question

襪 **maht** sock

密碼 **maht máh** password

米黃色 **máih wòhng sīk** beige

蚊 **mān** Hong Kong currency

乜野 **māt yéh** what

微波爐 **mèih bō lòuh** microwave

美國 **méih gwok** United States (U.S.)

美國人 **méih gwok yàhn** American

美元 **méih yùhn** dollar (U.S.)

名 **méng** name

棉花 **mìhn fā** cotton

明信片 **mìhn seun pín** postcard

棉條 **mìhn tíu** tampon
面 **mihn** face
麵包鋪 **mihn bāau póu** bakery
面部 **mihn bouh** facial
免費 **mín fai** free
免稅 **mín seui** duty-free
網吧 **móhng bā** internet cafe
網球 **móhng kàuh** tennis
剝 **mōk** v extract (tooth)
帽 **móu** hat
毛巾 **mòuh gān** towel
無限次使用嘅 **mòuh haahn chi sí yuhng ge** multiple-trip (ticket)
無酒精 **mòuh jáu jīng** non-alcoholic
無脂肪 **mòuh jī fōng** fat free
無聊嘅 **mòuh lìuh ge** boring
無味 **mòuh meih** bland
無線電話 **mòuh sin dihn wá** wireless phone
無線互聯網 **mòuh sin wuh lyùhn móhng** wireless internet
無線互聯網服務 **mòuh sin wuh lyùhn móhng fuhk mouh** wireless internet service
毛衣 **mòuh yī** sweater
無鉛 **mòuh yùhn** unleaded (gas)
冇 **móuh** without
舞蹈俱樂部 **móuh douh kēui lohk bouh** dance club

冇知覺 **móuh jī gok** unconscious
冇乜野 **móuh māt yéh** nothing
無人睇 **móuh yàhn tái** unattended
木炭 **muhk taan** charcoal
每 **múih** per
每個鐘頭 **múih go jūng tàuh** per hour
每個星期 **múih go sīng kèih** per week
每週 **múih jāu** weekly
每晚 **múih máahn** per night
每日 **múih yaht** per day

N

南 **nàahm** south
男仔 **nàahm jái** boy
男朋友 **nàahm pàhng yáuh** boyfriend
男人 **nàahm yán** man
難睇 **nàahn tái** ugly
奶粉 **náaih fán** formula (baby)
奶嘴 **náaih jéui** pacifier [soother BE]
奶樽 **náaih jēung** baby bottle
扭傷 **náu sēung** sprain
你好 **néih hóu** hello
女服務員 **néuih fuhk mouh yùhn** waitress
女仔 **néuih jái** girl

女裝恤衫 **néuih jōng sēut sāam** blouse

女朋友 **néuih pàhng yáuh** girlfriend

女人 **néuih yán** woman

顏色 **ngàahn sīk** color

眼 **ngáahn** eye

眼鏡 **ngáahn géng** glasses (optical)

硬幣 **ngaahng beih** coin

額外 **ngaak ngoih** extra

晏晝 **ngaan jau** noon [midday BE]

牙 **ngàh** tooth

牙膏 **ngàh gōu** toothpaste

牙醫 **ngàh yī** dentist

銀 **ngàhn** silver

銀包 **ngàhn bāau** purse; wallet

銀行 **ngàhn hòhng** bank

危險 **ngàih hím** dangerous

嘔 **ngáu** v vomit

牛仔布 **ngàuh jái bou** denim

牛仔褲 **ngáuh jái fu** jeans

午餐 **ngh chāan** lunch

午夜 **ngh yeh** midnight

餓 **ngoh** hungry

臥鋪車 **ngoh pōu chē** sleeper [sleeping BE] car

樂隊 **ngohk déui** orchestra

昂貴 **ngòhng gwai** expensive

愛 **ngoi** n/v love (someone)

愛爾蘭 **ngoi yíh làahn** Ireland

愛爾蘭人 **ngoi yíh làahn yàhn** Irish

外面 **ngoih mihn** outside

外套 **ngoih tou** coat

安全 **ngōn chyùhn** safe (protected)

安靜 **ngōn jihng** quiet

按 **ngon** v push

按摩 **ngon mō** massage

屋 **ngūk** house

呢 **nī** this

呢度 **nī douh** here

年 **nìhn** year

年輕 **nìhn hīng** young

年齡 **nìhn nìhng** age

尿 **niuh** urine

尿片 **niuh pín** diaper [nappy BE]

農產品 **nùhng cháan bán** produce

農產品商店 **nùhng cháan bán sēung dim** produce store

農場 **nùhng chèuhng** farm

暖 **nyúhn** adj/v warm

O

澳洲 **ou jāu** Australia

P

棒球 **páahng kàuh** baseball

排球賽 **pàaih kàuh choi** volleyball game

烹調 **pāang tìuh** v cook

跑馬場 **páau máh chèuhng** horse track

扒艇 **pàh téhng** rowboat

爬山電單車 **pàh sāan dihn dāan chē** mountain bike

貧血 **pàhn hyut** anemic

朋友 **pàhng yáuh** friend

噴髮劑 **pan faat jāi** hairspray

噴水池 **pan séui chìh** fountain

平 **pèhng** cheap

皮 **péi** leather

屁股 **pei gú** buttocks

皮帶 **pèih dáai** belt

皮膚 **pèih fū** skin

平底鑊 **pìhng dái wohk** saucepan

片 **pin** slice (of something)

票 **piu** ticket

膀胱 **pòhng gwōng** bladder

抱歉 **póu hip** sorry

普通 **póu tūng** regular

鋪位 **pou wái** berth

葡萄園 **pòuh tòuh yùhn** vineyard

配菜 **pui choi** side dish

S

沙漠 **sā mohk** desert

砂鍋 **sā wō** clay pot

曬傷 **saai sēung** sunburn

山 **sāan** mountain

刪除 **sāan chèuih** v delete

山頂 **sāan déng** peak (of a mountain)

山洞 **sāan duhng** cave

山仔 **sāan jái** hill

山路小徑 **sāan louh síu ging** trail

山路圖 **sāan louh tòuh** trail map

散紙 **sáan jí** change (money)

生日 **sāang yaht** birthday

殺蟲劑 **saat chùhng jāi** insect repellent

腎臟 **sahn johng** kidney (body part)

十字路口 **sahp jih louh háu** intersection

西部 **sāi bouh** west

西服套裝 **sāi fuhk tou jōng** suit

洗 **sái** v clean

洗潔精 **sái git jīng** dishwashing liquid

洗過嘅衫 **sái gwo ge sāam** laundry

洗頭水 **sái tàuh séui** shampoo

洗碗機 **sái wún gē** dishwasher

洗衣店 **sái yī dim** laundormat [launderette BE]

洗衣店設施 **sái yī dim chit sī** laundry facility

洗衣服務 **sái yī fuhk mouh** laundry service

洗衣機 **sái yī gēi** washing machine

細蚊仔 **sai mān jái** child

心口 **sām háu** chest (body part)

心口針 **sām háu jām** brooch

心口痛 **sām háu tung** chest pain

心臟 **sām johng** heart

心臟狀況 **sām johng johng fong** heart condition

森林 **sām làhm** forest

申報 **sān bou** v declare

新手 **sān sáu** novice (skill level)

新鮮 **sān sīn** fresh

失去 **sāt heui** lost

失物認領處 **sāt maht yihng líhng chyu** lost and found

失眠 **sāt mìhn** insomnia

室外游泳池 **sāt ngoih yàuh wihng chìh** outdoor pool

室內泳池 **sāt noih wihng chìh** indoor pool

膝頭 **sāt tàuh** knee

失業者 **sāt yihp jé** unemployed

修道院 **sāu douh yún** monastery

收費 **sāu fai** n charge (cost)

收據 **sāu geui** receipt

修腳趾甲 **sāu geuk jí gaap** pedicure

修理 **sāu léih** v fix (repair)

修手甲 **sāu sáu gaap** manicure

手 **sáu** hand

手臂 **sáu bei** arm

手錶 **sáu bīu** watch

手動汽車 **sáu duhng hei chē** manual car

手機 **sáu gēi** cell [mobile BE] phone

手掙 **sáu jāang** elbow

手指 **sáu jí** finger

手扼 **sáu ngáak** bracelet

首飾 **sáu sīk** jewelry

手提行李 **sáu tàih hàhng léih** carry-on [hand luggage BE]

手提箱 **sáu tàih sēung** suitcase

手推車 **sáu tēui chē** cart (grocery store)

手腕 **sáu wún** wrist

售票處 **sauh piu chyu** ticket office

寫 **sé** v write

錫 **sek** v kiss

醒 **séng** v wake

純銀 **sèuhn ngán** sterling silver

需要 **sēui yiu** v need

水池 **séui chìh** pool

水底呼吸設備 **séui dái fū kāp chit beih** snorkeling equipment

水晶 **séui jīng** crystal

睡袋 **seuih dói** sleeping bag

睡意 **seuih yi** drowsiness

睡衣 **seuih yī** pajamas

訊問處 **sēun mahn chyu**

information desk

信封 **seun fūng** envelope

信件 **seun gín** letter

信息 **seun sīk** information (phone); message

信用卡 **seun yuhng kāat** credit card

箱 **sēung** box

商場 **sēung chèuhng** shopping mall [shopping centre BE]

雙程 **sēung chìhng** round-trip [return BE] (ticket)

商店目錄 **sēung dim muhk luhk** store directory

相反 **sēung fáan** opposite

傷口 **sēung háu** n cut (injury)

商務 **sēung mouh** business

商務艙 **sēung mouh chōng** business class

傷心 **sēung sām** sad

雙人床 **sēung yàhn chòhng** double bed

商業中心 **sēung yihp jūng sām** business center

相 **séung** photo

相機 **séung gēi** camera

相機套 **séung gēi tou** camera case

想嘔 **séung ngáu** nauseous

恤衫 **sēut sāam** shirt

絲綢 **sī chàuh** silk

CD **sī dī** CD

絲巾 **sī gīn** scarf

試吓 **si háh** v taste

絲襪 **sī maht** pantyhose

使用 **sí yuhng** v use

試身室 **si sān sāt** fitting room

市場 **síh chèuhng** market

市地圖 **síh deih tòuh** town map

時間 **sìh gaan** time

時間表 **sìh gaan bíu** schedule [timetable BE]

時裝店 **sìh jōng dim** clothing store

市政廳 **síh jing tēng** town hall

市中心 **síh jūng sām** downtown

市中心廣場 **síh jūng sām gwóng chèuhng** town square

食 **sihk** v eat

食物 **sihk maht** food

食藥 **sihk yeuhk** v take

食煙 **sihk yīn** v smoke; smoking (area)

城堡 **sìhng bóu** castle

乘客 **sìhng haak** passenger

舌 **siht** tongue

熄 **sīk** turn off (lights)

適合 **sīk hahp** fit (clothing)

線 **sin** line (train)

星期 **sīng kèih** week

攝氏 **sip sih** Celsius

攝影器材商店 **sip yínghei**

chòih sēung dim camera store

燒 **sīu** v burn

消毒藥膏 **sīu duhk yeuk gōu** antiseptic cream

消防隊 **sīu fòhng yùhn** fire department

銷售稅 **sīu sauh seui** sales tax

小 **síu** small

小酒吧 **síu jáu bā** mini-bar

小組 **síu jóu** group

小溪 **síu kāi** stream

小路 **síu louh** trail [piste BE]

小路路線圖 **síu louh louh sin tòuh** trail [piste BE] map

小時 **síu sìh** hour

小食店 **síu sihk dim** snack bar

少少 **síu síu** little

梳 **sō** comb; hairbrush

炒鍋 **sō wō** wok

鎖 **só** n lock

鑰匙 **só sìh** key

鑰匙卡 **só sìh kāat** key card

鑰匙扣 **só sìh kau** key ring

桑拿 **sōng nàh** sauna

鬚後水 **sōu hauh séui** aftershave

帚把 **sou bá** broom

數字 **sou jih** number

數碼 **sou máh** digital

數碼相機 **sou máh séung gēi** digital camera

數碼相片 **sou máh seung pín** digital photo

數碼印刷品 **sou máh yan chaat bán** digital print

掃描器 **sou mìuh hei** scanner

素食者 **sou sihk jé** vegetarian

熟食 **suhk sihk** delicatessen

宿醉 **sūk jeui** hangover

宿舍 **sūk se** dormitory

送 **sung** v send

書 **syū** book

書店 **syū dim** bookstore

書法用品 **syū faat yuhng bán** calligraphy supplies

樹 **syuh** tree

船 **syùhn** boat

孫 **syūn** grandchild

損傷 **syún sēung** v damage

說唱樂 **syut cheung lohk** rap (music)

雪櫃 **syut gwaih** freezer

雪靴 **syut hēu** snowshoe

雪茄 **syut kā** cigar

T

太 **taai** too

太熟 **taai suhk** overdone

太陽 **taai yèuhng** sun

太陽眼鏡 **taai yèuhng ngáahn géng** sunglasses

探病時間 **taam behng sìh gaan** visiting hours

塔 **taap** tower
睇 **tái** v look
體操 **tái chōu** gym
睇見 **tái gin** v see
體育 **tái yuhk** sports
體育場 **tái yuhk chèuhng** stadium
體育用品商店 **tái yuhk yuhng bán sēung dim** sporting goods store
剃鬚刀 **tai sōu dōu** razor blade
剃鬚膏 **tai sōu gōu** shaving cream
吞 **tān** v swallow
偷 **tāu** v steal
偷竊 **tāu sit** theft
頭 **tàuh** head (body part)
頭等艙 **tàuh dáng chōng** first class
頭髮 **tàuh faat** hair
頭盔 **tàuh kwāi** helmet
投訴 **tàuh sou** complaint
頭痛 **tàuh tung** headache
頭暈眼花 **tàuh wàhn ngáahn fā** dizzy
推薦 **tēui jin** recommendation
腿 **téui** leg
退出 **teui chēut** v withdraw
退房 **teui fóng** check-out (hotel)
退休 **teui yāu** retired
T恤 **tī sēut** T-shirt
甜 **tìhm** sweet (taste)
填寫 **tìhn sé** v fill out (form)
停車 **tìhng chē** v park
停車場 **tìhng chē chèuhng** parking lot [car park BE]
停車計時器 **tìhng chē gai sìh hei** parking meter
停低 **tìhng dāi** v stop
天氣 **tīn hei** weather
聽日 **tīng yaht** tomorrow
聽力唔好 **ting lihk m hóu** hearing impaired
鐵軌 **tit gwái** track (train)
跳舞 **tiu móuh** v dance
拖車 **tō chē** tow truck
拖鞋 **tō háai** slippers
糖尿病 **tòhng niuh behng** diabetic
檯 **tói** table
托運 **tok wahn** v check (luggage)
湯羹 **tōng gāng** ceramic spoon
熨 **tong** v press (clothing)
熨斗 **tong dáu** n iron
熨衫 **tong sāam** v iron
肚屙 **tóu ngō** diarrhea
陶器 **tòuh hei** pottery
圖書館 **tòuh syū gún** library
同 **tùhng** with
銅 **tùhng** copper
同事 **tùhng sih** colleague
同一 **tùhng yāt** same

通知 **tūng jī** v notify
痛 **tung** pain
斷開 **tyúhn hōi** disconnect (computer)

W

還 **wàahn** v return
滑浪板 **waaht lohng báan** surfboard
滑水板 **waaht séui báan** water skis
壞咗 **waaih jó** damaged
玩 **wáan** v play
運動場 **wahn duhng chèuhng** field (sports)
運動鞋 **wahn duhng hàaih** sneaker
運動衫 **wahn duhng sāam** sweatshirt
暈浪 **wàhn lohng** travel sickness
運送 **wahn sung** v ship (mail)
餵 **wai** v feed
餵母乳 **wai móuh yúh** breastfeed
胃 **waih** stomach
為咗 **waih jó** for
衛生棉 **waih sāng mìhn** sanitary napkin [pad BE]
維生素 **wàih sāng sou** vitamin
胃痛 **waih tung** stomachache

溫泉 **wān chyùhn** hot spring
溫泉 **wān chyùhn** spa
V領 **wī léhng** V-neck
泳衣 **wihng yī** swimsuit
黃色 **wòhng sīk** yellow
污糟 **wū jōng** dirty
湖 **wùh** lake
護髮素 **wuh faat sou** conditioner
護照 **wuh jiu** passport
護照管制 **wuh jiu gún jai** passport control
互聯網 **wuh lyùhn móhng** internet
互聯網服務 **wuh lyùhn móhng fuhk mouh** internet service
護士 **wuh sih** nurse
換車 **wuhn chē** v change (buses)
換錢 **wuhn chín** v change (money)
換地方 **wuhn deih fōng** v exchange (place)
玩具店 **wuhn geui dim** toy store
玩具 **wuhn geuih** toy
換尿片 **wuhn niuh pín** v change (baby)
換現金 **wuhn yihn gām** v cash
回收 **wùih sāu** recycling
會係 **wúih haih** v be
會員證 **wúih yùhn jing** membership card

會議 **wuih yíh** conference; meeting

會議室 **wuih yíh sāt** meeting room

會議廳 **wuih yíh tēng** convention hall

碗 **wún** bowl

Y

任何野 **yahm hòh yéh** anything

人民幣 **yàhn màhn baih** Ren Min Bi (Chinese currency)

入場 **yahp chèuhng** admission

入口 **yahp háu** entrance

日 **yaht** day

日期 **yaht kèih** date (calendar)

陰道 **yām douh** vagina

陰道傳染 **yām douh chyùhn yíhm** vaginal infection

陰莖 **yām ging** penis

音樂 **yām ngohk** music

音樂商店 **yām ngohk sēung dim** music store

音樂廳 **yām ngohk tēng** concert hall

音樂會 **yām ngohk wúi** concert

飲 **yám** v drink

飲料 **yám liuh** n drink

飲料單 **yám liuh dāan** drink menu

飲用水 **yám yuhng séui** drinking water

隱形眼鏡 **yán yìhng ngáahn géng** contact lens

隱形眼鏡液 **yán yìhng ngáahn géng yihk** contact lens solution

一打 **yāt dā** dozen

一共 **yāt guhng** total (amount)

一樓 **yāt láu** ground floor

休息得好好 **yāu sīk dāk hóu hóu** well-rested

休息室 **yāu sīk sāt** restroom [toilet BE]

油 **yàuh** oil

遊蕩者 **yàuh dong jé** loafers

郵寄 **yàuh gei** v mail

郵件 **yàuh gín** n mail [post BE]

郵局 **yàuh gúk** post office

遊戲 **yàuh hei** game

遊戲圍欄 **yàuh hei wàih làahn** playpen

遊覽 **yàuh láahm** excursion; tour

遊覽勝地 **yàuh láahm sing deih** attraction (place)

遊樂園 **yàuh lohk yùhn** amusement park

郵票 **yàuh piu** n stamp (postage)

游水 **yàuh séui** v swim

郵箱 **yàuh sēung** mailbox [postbox BE]

猶太教堂 **yàuh taai gaau tóng** synagogue

猶太食品 **yàuh taai sihk bán** kosher

有趣 **yáuh cheui** interesting

有空房 **yáuh hūng fóng** vacancy

有咗 **yáuh jó** pregnant

有早餐嘅酒店 **yáuh jóu chāan ge jáu dim** bed and breakfast

有吸引力嘅 **yáuh kāp yáhn lihk** attractive

有遠見 **yáuh yúhn gin** far-sighted [long-sighted BE]

野餐區 **yéh chāan kēui** picnic area

夜 **yeh** night

夜總會 **yeh júng wúi** nightclub

夜晚 **yeh máahn** evening

藥房 **yeuhk fòhng** pharmacy [chemist BE]

藥方 **yeuhk fōng** prescription

藥膏 **yeuhk gōu** cream (ointment)

弱視者 **yeuhk sih jé** visually impaired

藥丸 **yeuhk yún** tablet (medicine)

羊毛 **yèuhng mòuh** wool

氧氣治療 **yéuhng hei jih lìuh** oxygen treatment

約 **yeuk** appointment

衣物 **yī maht** clothing

衣物櫃 **yī maht gwaih** locker

醫生 **yī sāng** doctor

醫藥 **yī yeuhk** medicine

醫院 **yī yún** hospital

意外 **yi ngoih** accident

以前 **yíh chìhn** before

胰島素 **yìh dóu sou** insulin

兒科醫生 **yìh fō yī sāng** pediatrician

兒童菜單 **yìh tùhng choi dāan** children's menu

兒童飯量 **yìh tùhng faahn leuhng** children's portion

兒童泳池 **yìh tùhng wìhng chìh** kiddlie [paddling BE] pool

宜家 **yìh gā** now

以後 **yíh hauh** after; later

耳仔 **yíh jái** ear

耳仔痛 **yíh jái tung** earache

耳筒 **yíh túng** headphones

耳環 **yíh wáan** earrings

嚴肅 **yìhm sūk** serious

驗光師 **yìhm gwōng sī** optician

現金 **yihn gām** n cash

營地 **yìhng deih** campsite

研討會 **yìhng tóu wúi** seminar

營業時間 **yìhng yihp sìh gaan** business hours

熱 **yiht** hot (temperature)